The 100 Greatest Rock Bassists

The 100 Greatest Rock Bassists

By

Greg Prato

Written by Greg Prato
Printed and distributed by Greg Prato Writer, Corp
Published by Greg Prato Writer, Corp
Front cover photo, back cover photo, intro photo, and front
cover design by Mary Prato

ISBN: 978-1723510205

Intro

To a large degree, it appears as though bass guitarists receive - to borrow a line from the legendary Rodney Dangerfield - "no respect." Just think - how many times have music publications or sites compiled a "greatest bassists" list, compared to "greatest vocalists" or "greatest guitarists" lists? The answer can be measured from about infrequent to zilch.

Perhaps this is because many do not think of the bass as a lead instrument. But bassists throughout the world know what certain unenlightened doofuses do not - the instrument is *crucial* to rock music. And in the right hands, the bass can spruce up a tune, and even serve as a key element in some of the greatest rock compositions ever (case in point, "My Generation," "Come Together," "Money," "Under Pressure," "For Whom the Bell Tolls," "Jeremy," etc.).

While there are a handful of bassists that even casual rock listeners could probably list as the cream of the crop, there are a whole lotta other talented players that brought new approaches to the party and/or put their own unique spin on the instrument, that may not be on the tip of many people's tongues. Which led to a realization by yours truly - who would the top 100 rock bassists of all-time be, based on a combination of how original their playing was, their contribution to the instrument, and their influence on other players? And to add to all the excitement, what if I did ten exclusive interviews (not confined to a wordcount), with some of rock's top bassists?

Lastly, a note about the book's set-up - I started from the bottom and worked my way to the top, and for each entry, there are five items - **Story** (a bit of background about what makes the specific player so darn special), **Standouts** (five songs which give the best examples of the player's bass skills), **Similar** (five bassists that...well, you know the rest), **Instruments** (several bass makes/models that the player has been most associated with), and **Pick or Fingers** (if the player prefers utilizing a plectrum or digits). And I opted not to include a table of contents at the beginning of the book, as it would spoil the surprise (and the building of excitement) as to who the top picks were...so you will find the complete list right after the winner is declared, followed by a list of honorable mentions and the aforementioned bassist interviews.

So, now that we've gotten that out of the way, it's time to embark on a journey regarding who I - and I'm quite confident many others - feel are the 100 greatest rock bassists!

Keep on thumping, slapping, popping, and plucking,
Greg Prato

p.s. Questions? Comments? Feel free to email me at this address - gregprato@yahoo.com.

Contents

The Countdown

101.
(this book goes to 101!)
Derek Smalls
(Spinal Tap)

Story: I know, I know, Spinal Tap was a goof and wasn't a real band. But...*so what?* Their bassist Derek Smalls (played by actor Harry Shearer) did a marvelous job poking fun at heavy metal bassists of the '80s and beyond in the classic 1984 comedy, *This is Spinal Tap.* But the main reason why it's crucial that Mr. Smalls receive his own entry in this little old book is because some of his basslines are simply stupendous (only two words are required to back this bold claim - "Big Bottom"). And who else would have been clever - or dimwitted - enough to suggest, and then embark upon, a free-form jazz exploration...*in front of a festival crowd?*

Standouts: "Big Bottom," "Heavy Duty," "Rock and Roll Creation," "Stonehenge," "Jazz Odyssey"

Similar: Gene Simmons, Blackie Lawless, Geezer Butler, Joey DeMaio, Steve Dawson

Instruments: BC Rich Eagle, BC Rich Doubleneck

Pick or Fingers: Fingers

100.
Richard Hell
(Richard Hell and the Voidoids)

Story: First wave punk (Stooges, New York Dolls, Ramones, etc.) was not exactly known for spawning bass heroes. But perhaps the closest out of the initial crop was Richard Hell (real name - Richard Meyers). An early member of the notoriously drug-addled Johnny Thunders and the Heartbreakers, it was not until Hell formed his own band, Richard Hell and the Voidoids (which included one of rock's most underrated guitarists, Robert Quine, plus eventual Ramones drummer Marky Ramone, then known as Marc Bell) that punkers worldwide took note.

And while it's Hell's lyrics that many fixate on (he was one of punk's first poets - along with Patti Smith), he was capable of composing bubbly basslines (although admittedly, often sounding like they were going to fall apart at any second) - especially on "Downtown at Dawn." You have to also give Hell additional props for helping trailblaze the "spikey hair look" (*before* Sid Vicious popularized it), and may have been the first rocker to rock "ripped clothing" fashion, too. Lastly, Hell has proven to be an inspiration and influence on quite a few subsequent notable bassists - tops on the list being Mike Watt.

Standouts: "Downtown at Dawn," "The Kid with the Replaceable Head," "Destiny Street," "Liars Beware," "Another World"

Similar: Glen Matlock, Dave Alexander, Arthur Kane, Fred Smith, Mike Watt

Instruments: Fender Mustang, Danelectro DC Cooper, Ampeg Dan Armstrong Lucite

Pick or Fingers: Fingers

99.
Glen Matlock
(Sex Pistols)

Story: Although Sid Vicious is probably the most talked about member of the Sex Pistols (for entirely non-musical reasons), one of the most important musical contributors to the band was his predecessor, Glen Matlock. Case in point, he co-authored (with the rest of the band) ten of the twelve tracks on the Pistols' lone - yet extremely classic/influential - debut album, 1977's *Never Mind the Bollocks...Here's the Sex Pistols*. One itty-bitty problem though - Matlock actually appears on only one tune on the entire record ("Anarchy in the UK"), as he had exited the band before the album's recording, and guitarist Steve Jones handled the majority of the album's bass work.

But if you inspect such non-official releases as *Spunk* - which comprises earlier demos of most of the *Bollocks* material, that Matlock plays on - you will hear that it was *he* who came up with the basslines that were later merely replicated (or in most cases, simplified) by Jones.

Supposedly, one of the reasons stated for Matlock's canning was because he was too darn musically talented - being one of the few punk bassists at the time to play with his fingers rather than going the way of the plectrum, and also for supposedly fancying the Beatles (a no-no among punk bands at the time). Matlock later dismissed these claims as malarkey, and was welcomed back into the Pistols for their on-again/off-again reunion shows in the late '90s/early 21st century.

Standouts: "Anarchy in the UK," "God Save the Queen," "Pretty Vacant," "Problems," "Submission"

Similar: Dee Dee Ramone, Captain Sensible, Paul Simonon, Pete Farndon, Krist Novoselic

Instruments: Fender Precision, Rickenbacker 4001

Pick or Fingers: Fingers

98.
Dee Dee Ramone
(The Ramones)

Story: Johnny Ramone's buzzsaw/down-picked rhythm guitar work was the main sonic ingredient to the Ramones' trademark punk sound. But keeping pace right alongside him was bassist Dee Dee Ramone (real name - Doug Colvin). While he never dare attempted to indulge in a bass solo on a Ramones song, his contributions were still vital -

whether it be solely writing or co-writing some of their best-known tunes (including "Blitzkrieg Bop") or counting off the songs rather than the drummer (by swiftly shouting "one, two, three, four!", which often times did not reflect the pace of the song that was to be played). But probably tops of the Dee Dee's accomplishments was how many subsequent bassists he inspired - including just about every four-stringer in a punk band post-1976.

Standouts: "Blitzkrieg Bop," "Commando," "Pinhead," "53rd and 3rd," "Today Your Love, Tomorrow the World"

Similar: Arthur Kane, Richard Hell, Glen Matlock, Paul Simonon, Jeff Magnum

Instruments: Fender Precision

Pick or Fingers: Pick

97.
Paul Simonon
(The Clash)

Story: Upon careful research, it has been determined that the two most renowned "gap toothed" bassists of all-time would have to be Flea of the Red Hot Chili Peppers and...Paul Simonon of the Clash. And interestingly, it turns out that both bassists have roots that lay in punk rock and funky sounds (although admittedly, Flea would later *fully* merge punk and funk together).

But Simonon was one of the first punk bassists to also embrace reggae (as heard on a tune he wrote and sang on the landmark *London's Calling* album, "The Guns of Brixton"). Uncannily however, two of the Clash's best-known tunes/bass-heavy tracks did *not* feature Paul (Norman Watt-Roy of Ian Dury and the Blockheads is heard on "The Magnificent Seven," while Clash drummer Topper Headon multi-tasks on "Rock the Casbah"). But no need to fret, Mr. Simonon (who also later reappeared as part of electro-rockers Gorillaz), we still love you and fully appreciate your contributions to the instrument.

Standouts: "London Calling," "The Guns of Brixton," "White Riot," "This Is Radio Clash," "Know Your Rights"

Similar: Jah Wobble, Norman Watt-Roy, Bruce Foxton, Graham Maby, Glen Matlock

Instruments: Fender Precision

Pick or Fingers: Both

96.
Mark Evans &
Cliff Williams
(AC/DC)

Story: The only time in this book that I caved in and decided to include a pair of players in the same entry would be the two blokes responsible for providing the low-end for

AC/DC (up until the release of his book, anyway) - Mark Evans and Cliff Williams. Both Evans and Williams were virtually identical with their bass capabilities and style - which required to keep things as simple as possible, and follow whatever the Young brothers were playing on their respective Gibsons and Gretsches.

And there are countless instances where both proved how nicely the presence of bass guitar can help fatten up an already thick groove - in Evans' case, give a listen to "She's Got Balls," and for Williams, "Back in Black" is hard to beat. Perhaps more so than any other rock artist, AC/DC showed how important solid/simple basslines can be - especially when you just happen to be playing on some of the greatest rock n' roll tunes of all-time.

Standouts: Mark Evans - "Live Wire," "She's Got Balls," "Dirty Deeds Done Dirt Cheap;" **Cliff Williams** - "Sin City," "Back in Black," "Who Made Who"

Similar: Tom Hamilton, Dusty Hill, Roger Glover, Ian Hill, Nikki Sixx

Instruments: Mark Evans - Gibson Ripper, Fender Precision
Cliff Williams - Ernie Ball Music Man Stingray, Fender Precision, Steinberger GL2

Pick or Fingers: Pick (for both)

95.
Colin Greenwood
(Radiohead)

Story: There was a period of time circa the closing moments of the '90s where it seemed like Radiohead was going to take over the world. But then...they went a bit nutty. And kudos to them - while housewives in America many not be familiar with their catalog, their fanbase remains loyal and massive. However, throughout it all, bassist Colin Greenwood has played a major role. And Greenwood's four-string was probably best-heard on such early classic recordings as *The Bends, OK Computer,* and *Kid A.* While his bass does in fact lead the charge every so often ("Bones," "The National Anthem"), his tasteful lines most often seem to weave in and out of their songs ("Airbag," "Paranoid Android") - like one of those colorful, old fashioned potholders, that some of us were lucky to make in grade school art class.

Standouts: "The National Anthem," "Paranoid Android," "Airbag," "Bones," "Morning Bell"

Similar: Chris Wolstenholme, Guy Berryman, Stefan Olsdal, Alex James, Nikolai Fraiture

Instruments: Fender Precision, Fender Jazz

Pick or Fingers: Fingers

94.
Jesse F. Keeler
(Death from Above)

Story: Whenever it seems like there aren't any new, interesting, and different-sounding rock artists to discover, along comes one that defies the odds (it's happened time and time again over the years young kiddies, *trust me*). And in the early 21st century, one such band was Death from Above (sometimes known as "Death from Above 1979"), whose bass duties are provided by a chap by the name of Jesse F. Keeler.

Keeler is joined by only drummer/singer Sebastien Grainger in the band, and with it being quite "hip" at the time to be a band of only two members - the most obvious examples being the White Stripes and the Black Keys - DFA did not specialize in the same bluesy shtick that Jack and Meg or Dan and Pat did/do. Instead, they created a pretty original rock style - part noise punk and part melodicism (with some metal muscle added for good measure), yet all the while being driven by Keeler's massively distorted yet groovy basslines.

Standouts: "Virgins," "Trainwreck 1979," "Black History Month," "Go Home, Get Down," "Romantic Rights"

Similar: Nick Oliveri, Michael Shuman, Jared Warren, Mike Kerr, Lemmy

Instruments: Ampeg Dan Armstrong, Rickenbacker 4001

Pick or Fingers: Pick

93.
Doug Pinnick
(King's X)

Story: The 12-string bass is certainly a mammoth-sounding instrument - which can be utilized as a tool to both move air out of your speaker and fill up an awful lot of space. Case in point, Doug Pinnick's bass work with King's X. Although not necessarily the flashiest of bassists, Doug (who also goes by the mononym, "dUg") has come up with his fair share of standout basslines (particularly the one that kicks off the song "Out of the Silent Planet" - not to be confused with the album of the same name). And although he's a pick-player, on at least one instance, he put down the plectrum and slapped up some funk ("Everybody Knows a Little Bit of Something").

But most impressive is Pinnick's ability to create an absolutely *thunderous* bass tone - as heard on such heavy-duty rockers as "Dogman." And he's also one of the busiest gents in all of rock n' roll, as he has been spotted in a variety of bands outside of King's X (including KXM, Grinder Blues, Tres Mts., and Pinnick Gales Pridgen, among others), as well as issuing solo releases (both under the nom de plume, Poundhound, plus his own name).

Standouts: "Out of the Silent Planet," "Everybody Knows a Little Bit of Something," "Dogman," "Looking for Love," "Groove Machine"

Similar: James Jamerson, Tom Petersson, Jeff Ament, Monty Colvin, Kip Winger

Instruments: Hamer B12L Chapparal, Fender Precision, Yamaha Custom AES 12-string, Yamaha Custom AES 4-string, Schecter dUg Pinnick Baron-H Bass

Pick or Fingers: Pick

92.

Tom Petersson
(Cheap Trick)

Story: Cheap Trick's Tom Petersson will not be confused with Billy Sheehan any time soon for fretboard fireworks on the bass. But that said, he is responsible for creating - and popularizing - one of the more interesting-sounding augmentations to the instrument in recent times. I'm talking about the 12-string bass, which sounded positively thundering (especially live) on tunes in which Cheap Trick stretched out and jammed out a bit - especially "Need Your Love" and "Gonna Raise Hell."

Since CT guitarist Rick Nielsen was more of a rhythm player/songwriter, guitar solos were kept to a bare minimum…leaving plenty of room for Petersson to hammer on his Hamer. And in ensuing years, several notable rock bassists followed Petersson's lead and added a 12-string to their arsenal (namely Doug Pinnick of King's X and Jeff Ament of Pearl Jam, to name but a few).

Standouts: "Speak Now or Forever Hold Your Peace," "He's a Whore," "Need Your Love," "I Know What I Want," "Gonna Raise Hell"

Similar: Doug Pinnick, Jeff Ament, Ben Orr, Michael Anthony, Prescott Niles

Instruments: Waterstone TP-12, Hamer B-12A, Hamer B-12S

Pick or Fingers: Pick

91.
Klaus Flouride
(Dead Kennedys)

Story: Hardcore punk was not about knowing your way around an instrument, but rather, the message you had to scream about. And the Dead Kennedys' original singer, the seemingly always-agitated Jello Biafra, was the ultimate example of a gentleman who had a lot on his mind. But it turns out that there was a surprisingly stellar band of instrumentalists backing him - including bassist Klaus Flouride...which was surprisingly his real name (just pulling your leg, it's Geoffrey Lyall).

And while Klaus had no problem keeping up with the ferocious onslaught of such ragers as "Nazi Punks Fuck Off" and "Buzzbomb," it was on the slower-paced tunes that he really shined, especially when delivering memorable basslines on such DK classics as "Holiday in Cambodia,"

"California Über Alles," and "Let's Lynch the Landlord," and even offering up an improv bassline on "Night of the Living Rednecks" that wouldn't sound entirely out of place being offered up by a lounge band.

Standouts: "Holiday in Cambodia," "California Über Alles," "Pull My Strings," "When Ya Get Drafted," "Let's Lynch the Landlord"

Similar: Chuck Dukowski, Darryl Jenifer, Dee Dee Ramone, Glen Matlock, Paul Simonon

Instruments: Fender Jazz

Pick or Fingers: Pick

90.
Bruce Foxton
(The Jam)

Story: The Jam's Bruce Foxton just may be the most energetic rock bassist ever. Of course, you can take the easy way out and view some vintage live video footage of the band to confirm this fact - but you can even make this assumption by inspecting the Jam's classic studio recordings (case in point, "In the City," "Going Underground," etc.). But Bruce the bassist was not just all about adrenaline and hyperactivity - as heard on the killer vintage Motown groove he cooks up on "Town Called Malice."

And while discussing the Jam, it's impossible not to at least mention their knack for sporting snazzy threads (and also Foxton serving as an early embracer of "the mullet" hairstyle). While most of their punk counterparts were dressed in leather jackets and torn dungarees, Foxton and co. were snappily dressed like mods straight out of the '60s (a la Jimmy Cooper and his cronies from *Quadrophenia*). After the Jam's split in 1982 (at the height of their popularity in their homeland of England), Foxton performed with fellow punkers Stiff Little Fingers, as well as eventually reuniting with drummer Rick Buckler, in From the Jam.

Standouts: "Start!", "Going Underground," "In the City," "Absolute Beginners," "Strange Town"

Similar: Bruce Thomas, Jean-Jacques Burnel, Steve Garvey, Captain Sensible, Pete Quaife

Instruments: Fender Precision, Rickenbacker 4001, Gibson EB-2, Aria Pro II SB-1000

Pick or Fingers: Pick

89.

Bruce Thomas
(Elvis Costello and the Attractions)

Story: If you like your new wave bass playing with a bit of bounce, then the Elvis Costello and the Attractions'

recordings featuring Bruce Thomas are a must-hear. Thomas' basslines were consistently interesting and inspired, and featured throughout what I strongly believe was Costello's finest hour, 1978's *This Year's Model,* which put Thomas front and center on such classics as "Pump It Up" and "This Year's Girl."

Thomas would remain the bassist through the Attractions' on-again/off-again affiliation with Elvis throughout the years - until a messy divorce between the singer and bassist occurred during the late '90s (which led to no performance by the band when they were inducted into the Rock and Roll Hall of Fame in 2003...although Thomas and all of the other Attractions were in attendance that evening).

Standouts: "Pump It Up," "This Year's Girl," "The Beat," "Accidents Will Happen," "(What's So Funny 'Bout) Peace, Love and Understanding"

Similar: Graham Maby, Bruce Foxton, Pete Farndon, Sting, Tina Weymouth

Instruments: Fender Precision, Bass Centre Profile/Bruce Thomas Signature

Pick or Fingers: Fingers

88.
Robert Sledge
(Ben Folds Five)

Story: In the '90s, bands like Mudhoney, My Bloody Valentine, and Smashing Pumpkins reintroduced the awesome sounds of the Electro-Harmonix Big Muff Pi distortion pedal back into rock music. However, not many bassists were bold enough to plug in...until Ben Folds Five's Robert Sledge arrived. A member of a trio that completely omitted six-string guitar (they were instrumentally comprised of just piano, bass, and drums), Sledge certainly had oodles of room to fill with his gloriously distorted bass. And fill it up he did, especially on "One Angry Dwarf and 200 Solemn Faces" (which also contained some impressive speed metal type bass riffing towards the end) and "Army."

And while the trio was best known for piano pop (as evidenced by their hit single, "Brick"), Sledge's fuzzed-out bass tone seemingly had more in common sonically with doom metal. Although BF5 split in 2000, Sledge and his bandmates have reunited off and on a few times subsequently, and each time, he thankfully remembered to bring along his bass and Big Muff.

Standouts: "One Angry Dwarf and 200 Solemn Faces," "Army," "Battle of Who Could Care Less," "Kate," "Erase Me"

Similar: Dan Lilker, Jesse F. Keeler, John Entwistle, Cliff Burton, Matt Lukin

Instruments: Epiphone Les Paul, Kay K162

Pick or Fingers: Pick

87.
Ben Shepherd
(Soundgarden)

Story: Probably the most pissed-off looking bassist (while performing in front of an audience) to be featured in this book is Soundgarden's Ben Shepherd - no instrument, amp, or monitor was safe. But besides all of his on-stage grumpiness, Shepherd is quite an underrated bassist, as his Sabbath-y basslines proved crucial to such SG classics as "Slaves and Bulldozers," approached Tool territory on "Rowing," and was even bold enough to step forward and take a solo on "My Wave."

In addition to supplying some extremely memorable and rugged basslines, perhaps Shepherd's biggest asset to the band was his songwriting skills, as he is listed as the sole author of such standout SG tracks as "Somewhere," "Head Down," "Half," "An Unkind," and "Attrition." And besides his work with Soundgarden, Shepherd has been a member of other more "garage rock" sounding bands that are certainly worth inspecting, including Hater and Wellwater Conspiracy.

Standouts: "Jesus Christ Pose," "Slaves and Bulldozers," "Rowing," "My Wave," "Spoonman"

Similar: Krist Novoselic, Scott Reeder, Hiro Yamamoto, Nick Oliveri, Geezer Butler

Instruments: Fender Jazz, Fender Precision, Fender Telecaster, Rickenbacker 4001

Pick or Fingers: Both

86.
Mark Sandman
(Morphine)

Story: Few rock bassists of the '90s created as unique of a sound with the bass as Morphine's Mark Sandman did. And he did it all with two less strings than the average bass player! Instead of manning a traditional bass, he fashioned his own unusual instrument with only two strings tuned to a fifth, and instead of fretting the strings with his fingers, he utilized a slide.

And the result was a sound unlike most rock bands at the time - picture the perfect soundtrack for a seedy bar past midnight (a la *Barfly*) or a film noir, and you wouldn't be far off. Sadly, Sandman's recording career proved to be far too brief, as he died on stage during a performance with the band in Palestrina, Italy, on July 3, 1999.

Standouts: "Thursday," "Buena," "Honey White," "Super Sex," "Good"

Similar: Chris Ballew, Chris Wood, Les Claypool, Erik Sanko, Larry Taylor

Instruments: Homemade 2-string instrument

Pick or Fingers: Pick (and a slide, too!)

85.

Krist Novoselic
(Nirvana)

Story: I'm sure Krist Novoselic would be the first to tell you that he is not the most technically-talented bass player. But that said, it was his straight-ahead and instantly memorable basslines that anchored some of the most tide-turning rock n' roll tunes ever. And in several instances, it was his bass that led the charge - I'm talkin' 'bout such tunes as "Love Buzz," "Blew," and "Hairspray Queen," among others.

And he accomplished this all while boldly holding his pick between his thumb and middle finger, and playing what appeared to be mostly second-hand (and quite battered) instruments - proving once again that it's the talent and expressiveness a player possesses in his fingertips that matters most, and not necessarily flaunting the most expensive brand/model.

Standouts: "Love Buzz," "Dive," "Blew," "Sliver," "Lounge Act"

Similar: Matt Lukin, Kurt Danielson, Mike Mills, Kim Deal, Klaus Flouride

Instruments: Ibanez Black Eagle 2609B, Gibson Ripper, Gibson Thunderbird, Gibson RD Standard

Pick or Fingers: Pick

84.
Andrew Weiss
(Rollins Band, Ween, Gone)

Story: When singer Henry Rollins was assembling his first post-Black Flag band - which would be christened the Rollins Band - he didn't have to look far and wide for a rhythm section, as bassist Andrew Weiss and drummer Sim Cain were members of BF's guitarist Greg Ginn's all-instrumental side band, Gone. Similar in style and approach to that of Geezer Butler and Cliff Burton (i.e., playing with his fingers and adding a healthy helping of distortion and wah), Weiss provided the low notes for the group from 1987-1992, before working with and producing other artists (including a long affiliation with Ween).

Standouts: "Low Self Opinion" (Rollins Band), "What Do You Do" (Rollins Band), "Tearing" (Rollins Band), "The Whole Truth" (Wartime), "Get Gone" (Gone)

Similar: Geezer Butler, Cliff Burton, Ben Shepherd, Chuck Dukowski, Melvin Gibbs

Instruments: Fender Precision

Pick or Fingers: Fingers

83.

Peter Hook
(Joy Division, New Order)

Story: The bridge between punk rock and new wave could quite possibly be pinpointed to Joy Division, a frustratingly short-lived band (due to the suicide of singer Ian Curtis in 1980, on the eve of their first-ever US tour). And while it was Curtis' dark-yet-poetic lyrics that seem to be the main fixation of the band, their bassist, Peter Hook, could surely deliver a solid bass hook (pun intended).

For example, the soaring keyboard part of "Love Will Tear Us Apart" may be the most memorable musical element of the song, but Hook plunking away at the bass provides much-needed support, while his bass melody on "She's Lost Control" is absolutely haunting. And when the surviving members of JD opted to carry on as New Order, a stylistic shift was in order (towards more electro-dance sounds). But Hook's bass still played a prominent role from time to time, such as on a holdover from their JD daze, "Ceremony."

Standouts: "Love Will Tear Us Apart" (Joy Division), "Disorder" (Joy Division), "She's Lost Control" (Joy Division), "Ceremony" (New Order), "Age of Consent" (New Order)

Similar: Dave Allen, Adam Clayton, David J, Kim Deal, Colin Greenwood

Instruments: Yamaha BB 1200S, Shergold Marathon 6-string, Hondo II [Rickenbacker 4001 copy], Fender Precision, Hagstrom Viking

Pick or Fingers: Pick

82.
Jah Wobble
(Public Image Limited, Jah Wobble's Invaders of the Heart)

Story: When John Lydon (aka Johnny Rotten) exited the Sex Pistols in 1978, he certainly could have taken the easy way out, and launched another outfit that was a musical carbon copy. But to his credit, instead, he opted to get experimental and unpredictable, and formed Public Image Limited (often stylized as PiL). And when it came time to assemble the band, he chose a pal at the time with little previous bass experience, Jah Wobble (real name - John Wardle).

On the two PiL studio albums that Wobble appears on (1978's *First Issue* and 1979's *Metal Box* - which helped trailblaze a genre known as "post-punk"), Wobble's bass played a major role on such toe-tapping tunes as "Public Image" and "Memories." But after exiting PiL, Wobble experienced a stylistic makeover himself - embracing world music (as the leader of Jah Wobble's Invaders of the Heart) and soundscape-y sounds (his work with Marconi Union).

Standouts: "Public Image" (PiL), "Memories" (PiL), "Poptones" (PiL), "Socialist" (PiL), "Visions of You" (collaboration with Sinéad O'Connor)

Similar: Tina Weymouth, Adam Clayton, Aston Barrett, Bakithi Kumalo, Jeff Ament

Instruments: Ovation Magnum, Yamaha BB, Fender Precision

Pick or Fingers: Fingers

81.

Martyn LeNoble
(Porno for Pyros)

Story: When singer Perry Farrell announced that Jane's Addiction was going bye-bye in 1991, it proved to be extremely disappointing news, as it appeared that the band was on the cusp of becoming one of the world's top rock bands. But Perry's next outfit, Porno for Pyros, proved to be outstanding, as well - and showed that he had an uncanny knack for scouting exceptional bass talent, as Martyn LeNoble proved to be up to the task of measuring up to JA's Eric Avery.

Martyn's funky/groovy bass stylings are all over the group's classic self-titled recording from 1992, and on more than half of their underrated follow-up, *Good God's Urge,* issued four years later. However, Martyn seemed to vanish musically post-P4P - as the most publicity he's received since then is his marriage to actress Christina Applegate. And this is quite unfortunate, as he had already found his own unique voice on the instrument, and it would have been interesting to see where he could have taken it on further recordings with the band (who as of this book's writing, have never bothered getting around to "album #3"). The reason why Mr. LeNoble isn't higher up on the list? His frustratingly small body of work.

Standouts: "Porno for Pyros," "Meija," "Pets," "Bad Shit," "Blood Rag"

Similar: Peter Hook, Eric Avery, Flea, Les Claypool, Bill Gould

Instruments: Warwick Thumb

Pick or Fingers: Fingers

80.

Bob Daisley
(Ozzy Osbourne, Rainbow)

Story: Few rock bassists have either played bass on and/or contributed in the songwriting department on as many classic recordings as Bob Daisley has. Don't believe me? I have the proof! On the tippy top of the list would have to be not only supplying bass on Ozzy Osbourne's two studio albums with Randy Rhoads (1980's *Blizzard of Ozz* and 1981's *Diary of a Madman*), but also, co-writing almost every single track on both, including such classics as "I

Don't Know," "Crazy Train," and "Mr. Crowley," among others.

Daisley would continue an on-again/off-again relationship with John Michael Osbourne (including playing and/or writing on all of Ozzy's studio albums from 1983-1991), one of Rainbow's finest albums of the "Ronnie James Dio era" (1977's *Long Live Rock n' Roll*), countless Gary Moore releases (including the 1990 classic *Still Got the Blues*), and even a Black Sabbath recording (1987's *The Eternal Idol*), among others. And while he shies away from performing gymnastics on his instrument, you can't deny the killer groove ol' Bob lays down on Rainbow's "Gates of Babylon."

Standouts: "Gates of Babylon" (Rainbow), "Crazy Train" (Ozzy Osbourne), "No More Tears" (Ozzy Osbourne), "Believer" (Ozzy Osbourne), "Tonight" (Ozzy Osbourne)

Similar: Roger Glover, Phil Lynott, Jimmy Bain, David Ellefson, Jason Newsted

Instruments: Fender Precision, Gibson EB-3

Pick or Fingers: Pick

79.
Glenn Hughes
(Deep Purple, Trapeze, Black Country Communion)

Story: Let's be honest - Roger Glover played on Deep Purple's best-known tracks ("Smoke on the Water," "Highway Star," "Strange Kind of Woman," etc.), but often times, he seemed to blend into the background like beige wallpaper. However, the bassist who replaced him in the band, Glenn Hughes, certainly made his presence felt - and additionally, possessed a splendid set of pipes (some would say even stronger than the man who served as Purple's lead vocalist at the time, David Coverdale).

And Purple was not the only great band that Hughes has been associated with, as evidenced by his work in the early '70s with Trapeze, a brief fling with Black Sabbath in the '80s, and the modern day supergroup, Black Country Communion. But that said, Hughes' work with Purple was probably the best of his career, as his playing has never gotten as fiercely funky as it was on "Gettin' Tighter" (especially during the middle break-down section).

Standouts: "Gettin' Tighter" (Deep Purple), "This Time Around/Owed to G" (Deep Purple), "Burn" (Deep Purple), "Hold On" (Deep Purple), "Keepin' Time" (Trapeze)

Similar: John Paul Jones, Geezer Butler, Bob Daisley, Rudy Sarzo, Jimmy Haslip

Instruments: Fender Jazz, Rickenbacker 4001, Yamaha GH Signature, Nash JB-63

Pick or Fingers: Pick

78.

Michael Anthony
(Van Halen, Chickenfoot)

Story: How the heck do you make your presence felt in a band when your line-up features one of the undisputed greatest rock guitarists of all-time? That is precisely the complicated situation that Michael Anthony (real name - Michael Anthony Sobolewski) found himself in throughout his tenure as the bassist for Van Halen - playing alongside Eddie Van Halen. But to Mr. Anthony's credit, from the get-go, he knew his place in the band, and not only seemed to wholeheartedly accept it…but thrived in his "supporting player" role, while his stellar backing vocals proved to be a highly important ingredient to the =VH= sound (in fact, you could even make the argument he was a better singer than David Lee Roth!).

And in the process, Michael had more than a few opportunities to prove that he did indeed know his way around the instrument - case in point, the slip-sliding opening to "Push Comes to Shove," the repetitive single-note (yet quite iconic) start of "Runnin' with the Devil," etc. And Anthony stuck around long enough to be a part of several different line-up incarnations (the first two Roth eras, the two Sammy Hagar eras, and the best-forgotten lone Gary Cherone era), before controversially being replaced by EVH's son, Wolfgang, when Roth reclaimed his spot behind the mic in 2007. But instead of sitting around sulking, he reconnected with his old pal, Hagar, in Chickenfoot.

Standouts: "Push Comes to Shove," "So This Is Love?", "Runnin' with the Devil," "You're No Good," "Romeo Delight"

Similar: Tim Bogert, Roger Glover, Dusty Hill, Ian Hill, Cliff Williams

Instruments: Jack Daniel's Bass, Tabasco Bass, Yamaha BB3000MA, Schecter Michael Anthony, Rickenbacker 4001, Charvel Explorer

Pick or Fingers: Both

77.

Brian Wilson
(The Beach Boys)

Story: I know, I know, we all understand that Brian Wilson did not always play bass on Beach Boys records (session musician Carol Kaye is credited for supplying bass during the sublime *Pet Sounds* era, including "Sloop John B"). But that said, Wilson *wrote* the basslines that were played - in addition to composing countless classic pop gems. In fact, when you think of "surf music," the drenched-in-reverb bassline of "Good Vibrations" probably automatically comes to mind for many.

So, while he's not thought of first and foremost for his bass skills, including Mr. Wilson in this book would still be the right thing to do...don't you agree? And just to clarify - Brian could have been potentially far higher on his list...but since it's difficult to confirm which tunes he actually *played* bass on, I think including him here sounds about right.

Standouts: "Good Vibrations," "In My Room," "I Just Wasn't Made For These Times,' "Vegetables," "Don't Worry Baby"

Similar: Carol Kaye, Jerry Scheff, Paul McCartney, Bill Wyman, Donald "Duck" Dunn

Instruments: Fender Precision, Valley Arts California Pro, Sadowsky Precision

Pick or Fingers: Pick

76.
Phil Lesh
(Grateful Dead)

Story: If it's treble in your bass that you require, then the Grateful Dead's Phil Lesh just may be your main man - as evidenced by his meandering basslines throughout "Friend of the Devil." And while tagged a "jam band" by many - who specialized in seemingly never-ending jams in concert (hence the genre's name, duh!) - if I can speak from my personal taste, I always preferred the Dead's more succinct songwriting on their studio albums rather than their extended live recordings. Impressively, a wide range of bassists have listed Phil L as a big-time influence on their playing, including everyone from the Meat Puppets' Cris Kirkwood to Phish's Mike Gordon.

Standouts: "Friend of the Devil," "China Cat Sunflower," "Cumberland Blues," "Unbroken Chain," "Shakedown Street"

Similar: Jack Casady, Rick Danko, Berry Oakley, Cris Kirkwood, Mike Gordon

Instruments: Fender Jazz, Guild Starfire, Modulus Quantum 6-string, Alembic Series II 6-string, Alembic Custom

Pick or Fingers: Pick

75.
Tommy Shannon
(Stevie Ray Vaughan and Double Trouble, Johnny Winter)

Story: Similar to the aforementioned Michael Anthony/EVH situation, good luck getting noticed in a band when part of the line-up features the legendary Stevie Ray Vaughan on the six-string. But as one-half of Double Trouble, bassist Tommy Shannon offered up his fair share of funky and bluesy bass (and with the latter genre not exactly known for its basslines, it makes this an even more impressive accomplishment).

Case in point, while SRV is wailing away on the two standout instrumentals from 1983's *Texas Flood,* "Testify" and "Rude Mood," keep a close ear on Shannon and his bass. And because of his work with SRV (he appeared on all of his recordings from 1983-1989), it's easy to forget that Shannon was a member of another blues rock legend's band, Johnny Winter, once upon a time (appearing on his first two classic albums).

Standouts: "Testify" (Stevie Ray Vaughan and Double Trouble), "Rude Mood" (Stevie Ray Vaughan and Double Trouble), "Couldn't Stand the Weather" (Stevie Ray Vaughan and Double Trouble), "Scuttle Buttin'" (Stevie Ray Vaughan and Double Trouble), "I'm Not Sure" (Johnny Winter)

Similar: Billy Cox, John Paul Jones, Keith Ferguson, Dusty Hill, James Dewar

Instruments: Fender Jazz, Fender Precision

Pick or Fingers: Fingers

74.
Herbie Flowers
(Lou Reed, David Bowie)

Story: One of the most instantly-recognizable basslines in rock history is undoubtedly Lou Reed's "Walk on the Wild Side." However, the gent who played this smooth n' jazzy motif (which was concocted by double tracking an electric bass and stand-up bass together, by the way) remains unknown to many. Thankfully, in a book such as this, Herbie Flowers (real name - Brian Keith Flowers) finally gets his just desserts, that he so rightfully deserves.

And the reason why Flowers' name is not on the tip of many tongues is because he served as a session musician. But boy, did his basslines find their way on a number of classic rock gems, tops being David Essex's "Rock On," Harry Nilsson's "Jump into the Fire," and David Bowie's "Rebel Rebel," as well as one of the most bombastic prog rock tunes ever, Sky's "Toccata." And his go-to electric bass through it all was a well-weathered Fender Jazz, originally purchased from the now sadly-defunct Manny's Music in NYC, back in 1959.

Standouts: "Walk on the Wild Side" (Lou Reed), "Rock On" (David Essex), "Jump into the Fire" (Harry Nilsson), "Rebel Rebel" (David Bowie), "Toccata" (Sky)

Similar: John Paul Jones, Greg Lake, Jack Bruce, Tony Levin, Fernando Saunders

Instruments: Fender Jazz

Pick or Fingers: Both

73.
Trevor Bolder
(David Bowie and the Spiders from Mars, Uriah Heep)

Story: Despite all the over-the-top on-stage theatrics and shenanigans surrounding David Bowie and the Spiders from Mars during the early '70s, the band was comprised of remarkable musicians - including bassist Trevor Bolder.

With Bowie and guitarist Mick Ronson seemingly battling each other for the spotlight, Bolder let his fingers do the talking, as heard by his robust basslines featured on such classics as "The Jean Genie" and "John, I'm Only Dancing."

Additionally, during his time as a Spider, Bolder sported the most badass sideburns in all of rock. And after the Spiders went kerplunk after Bowie's *Aladdin Sane* album in 1973, Bolder did not remain idle for long. By '77, he had signed on with prog-metallists Uriah Heep, and manned his position in the band until his passing in 2013, at the age of 62.

Standouts: "The Jean Genie," "Moonage Daydream," "John, I'm Only Dancing," "Suffragette City," "Hang Onto Yourself"

Similar: Steve Currie, Pete Overend Watts, Suzi Quatro, Steve Priest, Jim Lea

Instruments: Gibson EB-O, Fender Precision

Pick or Fingers: Fingers

72.
Trevor Dunn
(Mr. Bungle, Fantômas)

Story: During the '90s, Faith No More vocalist Mike Patton made it quite known that he was also in another band, called Mr. Bungle (he actually sported a Bungle shirt in the FNM video for "Epic"). But unlike many other musical artists who utilize side bands as a light detour to merely blow off some creative steam, it turned out that Bungle was comprised of extremely talented musicians - who could handle everything from death metal and jazz improv to surf music and Middle Eastern sounds. And their bassist, Trevor Dunn, had no problem navigating through this treacherous stylistic terrain with his instrument.

Case in point, Dunn does his best Flea impersonation on "Squeeze Me Macaroni," and covers countless rotating styles throughout the everything-but-the-kitchen-sink composition, "Carry Stress in Jaw." And despite Bungle sadly being put into mothballs after the tour in support of their third album, 1999's *California,* was completed, Dunn has remained extremely busy, working furthermore with Patton in both Fantômas and Tomahawk, as well as with the Melvins, and exploring his jazzier side (albeit with sonic surprises/twists and turns) as the leader of Trevor Dunn's Trio-Convulsant.

Standouts: "Carry Stress in Jaw," "Egg," "Carousel," "Squeeze Me Macaroni," "Platypus"

Similar: Les Claypool, Flea, Bill Gould, Robert Trujillo, Jeff Pinkus

Instruments: Fender Precision, Alembic Europa 5-string, Ken Lawrence 5-string fretless

Pick or Fingers: Both

71.
Frank Bello
(Anthrax)

Story: It seemed like most thrash metal bassists of the '80s opted to play with a pick - which is understandable, due to the genre's breakneck tempos and the precision it takes to play their lines properly. But there were certainly exceptions - such as Anthrax's Frank Bello, who bravely opted to utilize his digits. Although he mostly anchored the guitar lines that the six-stringers were playing, there were certainly moments where he stepped up to the plate - such as a surprise metal makeover of Joe Jackson's new wave classic, "Got the Time" (complete with mid-song bass solo).

Standouts: "Got the Time," "Caught in a Mosh," "Efilnikufesin (NFL)," "Lone Justice," "One World"

Similar: Steve Harris, Robert Trujillo, David Ellefson, Joey Vera, Steve Di Giorgio

Instruments: Fender Frank Bello Signature, ESP Frank Bello Signature

Pick or Fingers: Fingers

70.

Dan Lilker
(Stormtroopers of Death, Nuclear Assault, Brutal Truth, Anthrax)

Story: Bass guitar and distortion are a glorious mixture (at least according to my ears, anyway) - which makes it puzzling as to why most bassists seem frightened of a little fuzz. But Dan Lilker has boldly incorporated distortion into his sound - especially throughout the classic 1985 debut by Stormtroopers of Death (aka SOD), *Speak English or Die.* Originally a member of Anthrax, the amazingly longhaired Lilker only appeared on the group's debut album, *Fistful of Metal,* before going on to focus on even heavier forms of metal - with the likes of Nuclear Assault and Brutal Truth.

For quite some time, I thought that Lilker would have been a good choice to replace Cliff Burton in Metallica (after Burton tragically passed away in 1986), due to both their fondness for the d-word. And when I had the opportunity to interview Lilker for Songfacts in 2014, I mentioned this tidbit, and he did admit that the thought had crossed his mind at the time...but he never received "the call." A missed opportunity for both sides, if you ask me.

Standouts: "Milk" (SOD), "Speak English or Die" (SOD), "Chromatic Death" (SOD), "Sargent 'D' and the SOD" (SOD), "Critical Mass" (Nuclear Assault)

Similar: Lemmy, Cliff Burton, Tom Araya, Pete Steele, Geezer Butler

Instruments: BC Rich Warlock, Warwick Streamer Stage I 4

Pick or Fingers: Pick

69.
David Ellefson
(Megadeth)

Story: Give Megadeth bassist David Ellefson credit - in addition to being in a band with Dave Mustaine for decades (which is no mean feat - just take a gander at the long list of Mega-members that have come and gone over the years), he also has no trouble keeping up with his rapid fire riffs. While the majority of thrash metal bassists seemingly played it safe and merely followed what the rhythm guitarist was playing, Ellefson certainly came up with basslines that ventured outside of the box - go ahead and give the relentless "Take No Prisoners" a test drive. And of course, he is responsible for playing one of the most instantly identifiable basslines in all of hard rock/heavy metal history, "Peace Sells" (aka, the long-time theme music for MTV News).

Standouts: "Peace Sells," "Holy Wars…the Punishment Due," "Take No Prisoners," "Dawn Patrol," "Symphony of Destruction"

Similar: Jason Newsted, Tom Araya, Frank Bello, DD Verni, Rex Brown

Instruments: Jackson David Ellefson CB-XV, Jackson David Ellefson CB-X, Jackson David Ellefson Signature Kelly Bird, BC Rich Mockingbird

Pick or Fingers: Pick

68.
Joey DeMaio
(Manowar)

Story: If you can look past the furry loincloth and He-Man/Conan the Barbarian shtick, Manowar's Joey DeMaio was quite the bass shredder back in the day. At the peak of the Manowar mountain of metal would be the bass-freakout-solo "Black Arrows," which was in line with what Billy Sheehan and Eddie Van Halen were doing at the time. But DeMaio also enjoyed laying down tranquil bass intros to songs, before the listener was met head-on with metal - including such tunes as "Battle Hymn." And Joey should be given additional salutation for playing unique instruments, such as a custom-made guitar (known as the Demon II), which features an ultra-thin, carbon fiber neck.

Standouts: "Black Arrows," "Battle Hymn," "Defender," "Gates of Valhalla," "Mountains"

Similar: Derek Smalls, Lemmy, Steve Harris, Peter Baltes, David Ellefson

Instruments: Rickenbacker 4001, Demon II, Veilette-Citron 8-string

Pick or Fingers: Pick

67.
Randy Coven

Story: With Billy Sheehan harvesting heaps of praise and media attention circa *Eat 'Em and Smile,* other bassists interested in utilizing the four-string as a lead instrument - and not bashful about showing off their stunning skills - also began to enjoy coverage. Case in point, Randy Coven. Although he never received the kind of accolades as say, Sheehan or Stu Hamm, Coven had just as much command over his instrument as the others. But, unlike those two specific bassists, Coven did not score a highly-coveted gig during the '80s that could have helped introduce his talents to the masses.

Still, Coven's abilities were recognized by others, as he crossed paths in the studio over the years with the likes of his old Berklee classmate (and fellow Long Island native) Steve Vai, plus Jeff Watson, Leslie West, Zakk Wylde, and Al Pitrelli, among others. And Randy was one of the few bassists (aside from Les Claypool) who truly made the whammy bar part of his sound, as well. Sadly, this underrated bassist would pass away at the age of 54, on May 20, 2014.

Standouts: "Funk Me Tender," "The Chase," "CPR," "Nu School," "Wah Song"

Similar: Stu Hamm, Billy Sheehan, Dave LaRue, Jeff Berlin, Beaver Felton

Instruments: Barrington [unsure of model], Ibanez [unsure of model], TZACK Fretless Artist Series Randy Coven Model, Warwick Stryker

Pick or Fingers: Fingers

66.
Darryl Jenifer
(Bad Brains)

Story: The late/great Bob Marley once sang a song entitled "Punky Reggae Party" - a phrase which could also be borrowed to describe the music of the Bad Brains. And the man supplying the low-end in the band was a tall chap with long dreadlocks, by the name of Darryl Jenifer. It turned out that like his bandmates, Jenifer had no problem rolling with the multitude of stylistic shifts thrown his way - whether it be explosive hardcore punk ("Sailin' On"), reggae ("I and I Survive"), heavy metal ("Soul Craft"), and funk (a cover of Larry Graham's "Hair") - played on a well-worn, aqua-colored instrument.

Standouts: "Voyage Into Infinity," "The Regulator," "The Youth are Getting Restless," "She's Calling You," "Banned in DC"

Similar: Paul Simonon, Klaus Flouride, Muzz Skillings, Aston Barrett, Larry Graham

Instruments: Modulus Bassstar

Pick or Fingers: Pick

65.
Cris Kirkwood
(Meat Puppets)

Story: Few rock bands transformed stylistically as much as the Meat Puppets did over the course of their first three albums - going from noise-punk (1982's self-titled debut) to country-punk (1984's *Meat Puppets II*), before winding up whirling in a pool of psychedelia (1985's *Up on the Sun*). And while the band's singer/guitarist/songwriter, Curt Kirkwood, tends to get the lion's share of attention for his six-string talents, his younger brother, Cris, is a highly underrated and outstanding bassist.

As the band's music began getting more complex and taking on a variety of styles, Cris' bass playing was able to adapt and branch out, as well. Case in point, the opening of the mostly-instrumental (except for whistling) "Maiden's Milk," in which the K-bros play a melody in unison, that wouldn't sound out of place being performed at a Renaissance Fair. But Cris' knack for memorable and surprisingly solid basslines didn't stop there, as his four-string work has served as a major presence on the majority of Puppets recordings (especially on such instrumentals as "Seal Whales" and "Six Gallon Pie").

Standouts: "Maiden's Milk," "Seal Whales," "Six Gallon Pie," "Up on the Sun," "Get On Down"

Similar: Dusty Hill, Phil Lesh, Mike Mills, Jeff Pinkus, Krist Novoselic

Instruments: Fender Precision, Steinberger XM

Pick or Fingers: Both

64.
Jeff Ament
(Pearl Jam, Temple of the Dog, Mother Love Bone)

Story: Fretless, funky (without slapping/popping), and groovy...while sometimes utilizing a 12-string. Certainly not a very common bass recipe within the world of rock during the early '90s. But then again, Jeff Ament is not your average/ordinary bassist. First rising up with proto-grungers Green River, before almost hitting the big-time with tragic glam-grungers Mother Love Bone, it was not until 1991/'92, with the emergence of Pearl Jam (and a one-off supergroup, Temple of the Dog), that Ament became one of rock's leading bassists. Additionally, Ament is also responsible for composing one of the most instantly recognizable rock basslines of all-time - of course, I'm talking about the massive sounding 12-string riff that opens up "Jeremy."

Standouts: "Jeremy," "Oceans," "Even Flow," "Rats," "Tremor Christ"

Similar: Doug Pinnick, Eric Avery, Hiro Yamamoto, Flea, Robert DeLeo

Instruments: Hamer USA B12A 12-string, Wal Bass Fretless MK 2, Mike Lull Jeff Ament JAXT4

Pick or Fingers: Both

63.
Eric Avery
(Jane's Addiction)

Story: If I had to vote for a rock bassist who came up with some of my favorite rock basslines of all-time in the *shortest* amount of time, I just may have to vote for Eric Avery. As the original bassist for Jane's Addiction, Avery created truly sturdy, to-the-point, and memorable bass bits circa the late '80s/early '90s (the original JA line-up split in 1991) - tops being "Up the Beach," "Ted, Just Admit It," "Summertime Rolls," and "Mountain Song."

Taking influences from both post-punk and funk, I also recall reading once that what supposedly helped Avery shape his bass style was that he constantly played acoustic guitar. Perhaps that is valuable advice for budding bassists? Either way, apart from a brief reconciliation with his JA mates for a tour in 2009, Avery has remained a much in-demand "bassist for hire," as evidenced by his work with

Nine Inch Nails, Garbage, Peter Murphy, and Alanis Morissette, as well as an unsuccessful tryout for Metallica, and close calls with both the Smashing Pumpkins and Nine Inch Nails. And I'd like to add an interesting aside concerning Mr. Avery - he always reminded me (looks-wise) of Duff McKagan from Guns N' Roses. Amusingly, in 2010, McKagan briefly occupied Avery's former position in JA.

Standouts: "Ted, Just Admit It," "Up the Beach," "Mountain Song," "Ain't No Right," "Been Caught Stealing"

Similar: Jeff Ament, Martyn LeNoble, Flea, Kim Deal, Duff McKagan

Instruments: Fender Precision, Fender Jazz

Pick or Fingers: Pick

62.
Bill Gould
(Faith No More)

Story: Like the band that he co-founded and is best known for being associated with, Faith No More bassist Bill Gould is impossible to pin down to a single style...but has no problem shape-shifting his playing to fit in. While his roots were in post-punk, goth, and new wave (which is evident throughout Faith No More's 1985 debut, *We Care a Lot*), his bass style eventually broadened to touch upon Middle

Eastern bits ("Falling to Pieces" and especially "Woodpecker from Mars"), extreme metal ("Surprise! You're Dead!" and "Malpractice"), and funk ("Epic" and "Anne's Song").

Although the dreaded "funk metal" tag has been attached to FNM and Gould at times, there is so much more to his playing than merely slapping and popping the night away. Also, when he has ventured away from FNM, he continued to embrace a variety of styles with other projects, including lending his bass skills to death metallists Brujeria and hardcore punkers Jello Biafra and the Guantanamo School of Medicine, among others. And it turns out that Gould has a keen business sense, as he is the long-time head honcho of an indie label, Koolarrow Records.

Standouts: "Epic," "Falling to Pieces," "Anne's Song," "Woodpecker from Mars," "Land of Sunshine"

Similar: Flea, Trevor Dunn, Peter Hook, Fieldy, Paulo Jr.

Instruments: Zon Sonus Custom 4

Pick or Fingers: Both

61.
Dave Allen
(Gang of Four)

Story: Can the bass guitar still be funky, while being paired with discordant guitar? You betcha! Just give a listen to the bass stylings of Dave Allen on the first two classic albums by Gang of Four - 1979's *Entertainment!* and 1981's *Solid Gold* - as Allen's Fender P-Bass continuously did battle with Andy Gill's slashing guitar lines. But as stated earlier, Go4 also managed to be quite funky, and Allen's bass playing in particular (without going the slap n' pop route as many funk bassists have gone - since Allen was a pick player).

After exiting the Gang in '81, Allen has reappeared as part of two other bands - Shriekback and King Swamp - while also reuniting with this old Go4 mates for a jiffy during the early 21st century (resulting in shows and an album of re-recordings, 2005's *Return the Gift*). Interestingly, in 2014, Beats Music hired Allen to be the company's public face and chief advocate.

Standouts: "Ether," "Not Great Men," "Damaged Goods," "At Home He's a Tourist," "What We All Want"

Similar: Jah Wobble, Peter Hook, Adam Clayton, Flea, Eric Avery

Instruments: Fender Precision

Pick or Fingers: Pick

60.
Adam Clayton
(U2)

Story: With Bono's vocals and the Edge's distinctive guitar stylings absorbing most of the spotlight in U2, Adam Clayton's simple-yet-effective basslines still managed to help drive things along. Case in point, such early classics as "I Will Follow" and "Gloria." And as heard in such tunes as "Exit" and "Lemon," Mr. Clayton could also certainly hold his own when the bass was required to stand up, front and center. And you have to give the man additional props for wielding one of the oddest shaped/colored basses of recent times - the Auerswald Adam Clayton Custom - which is affectionately often referred to as "The Banana Bass" (you'll understand why once you see it).

Standouts: "New Year's Day," "I Will Follow," "Gloria," "Exit," "Lemon"

Similar: Tony Butler, Phil Lynott, Mike Mills, Jeff Ament, Guy Berryman

Instruments: Fender Precision, Ibanez Musician, Warwick Adam Clayton Artist, Fender Jazz Bass Adam Clayton Signature, Auerswald Adam Clayton Custom, Warwick Custom Streamer CV

Pick or Fingers: Both

59.
Phil Lynott
(Thin Lizzy)

Story: Thin Lizzy will always be best remembered for Phil Lynott's poetic lyrics and the twin guitar harmonies of Scott Gorham and whichever other guitarist he was paired with at the time (the list is quite substantial). But it turns out that Lynott was also a solid bassist, as heard by his groovy lines on such Lizzy classics as "Dancing in the Moonlight (It's Caught Me in Its Spotlight)" and "Waiting for an Alibi," while stretching out a bit on his solo material, especially such compositions as "Solo in Soho" and "Talk in '79."

Standouts: "Dancing in the Moonlight (It's Caught Me in Its Spotlight)" (Thin Lizzy), "Waiting for an Alibi" (Thin Lizzy), "Emerald" (Thin Lizzy), "Fats" (Thin Lizzy), "Solo in Soho" (Phil Lynott)

Similar: Adam Clayton, Tony Butler, Pete Way, Glenn Hughes, Dusty Hill

Instruments: Fender Precision, Ibanez Roadster RS-900, Roland G-88, BC Rich Mockingbird

Pick or Fingers: Pick

58.
Gene Simmons
(Kiss)

Story: Kiss' make-up and costumes are instantly recognizable throughout the world - not to mention their extravagant stage show, also. And while it has brought them fame and fortune, it often gets in the way of the fact that the band has penned countless rock classics, which has contained some pretty darn solid musicianship, to boot. While guitarist Ace Frehley has been name-checked as a key influence by seemingly every rock guitarist from the mid '80s onward, Gene Simmons seems to be one of the principal gents (perhaps behind only Paul McCartney) that inspired many a rock bassist to first pick up the instrument.

Kiss' self-titled debut arrived in 1974, and the album is probably Kiss' most "bass-heavy." While the instrument leads the charge on one of the album's standout tracks, "100,000 Years," overall, Mr. Simmons' basslines are never flashy, but he does certainly know his way around the fretboard, as evidenced by the album's lone instrumental, "Love Theme from Kiss." And while he will not be mistaken for Stu Hamm any time soon, Simmons' tasteful playing has helped anchor some of Kiss' best known tracks, most obviously, the arena rock anthem, "Detroit Rock City."

Standouts: "100,000 Years," "She," "Love Theme from Kiss," "Cold Gin," "Detroit Rock City"

Similar: Roger Glover, Lemmy, Michael Anthony, Nikki Sixx, Krist Novoselic

Instruments: Gibson Grabber, Gibson Ripper, Spector (unsure of model), Kramer Axe, Pedulla MVP, Punisher

Pick or Fingers: Pick

57.

Roger Glover
(Deep Purple, Rainbow)

Story: Certainly one of the most *mammoth* sounding hard rock/heavy metal bands of all-time was Deep Purple - due to Ian Gillan's shrieking vocals, Ritchie Blackmore's genius killer riffs and solos, Jon Lord's blaring organ, Ian Paice's pounding percussion...and Roger Glover's solid bass. Although seemingly primarily thought of as a fellow who merely held the groove down on his four-string, Glover could occasionally be a snake hiding out in the grass, as evidenced by his bass solos on such rockers as "Fireball" and "Pictures of Home."

And just to be able to be a part of the greatest rock guitar riff of all-time, "Smoke on the Water" (OK, OK...maybe a two-way tie with "Iron Man"), automatically catapults Glover to elevated status. Besides his work with Purple, one mustn't also forget Glover's work with Rainbow, nor his remarkable production credentials (Judas Priest, David Coverdale, Michael Schenker Group, etc.).

Standouts: "Smoke on the Water," "Highway Star," "Pictures of Home," "Woman from Tokyo," "Fireball"

Similar: Mel Schacher, Felix Pappalardi, Bob Daisley, Jimmy Bain, Francis Buchholz

Instruments: Rickenbacker 4001, Fender Precision, Vigier Excess Roger Glover Custom

Pick or Fingers: Pick

56.
Mel Schacher
(Grand Funk)

Story: I think the best description of Grand Funk and their bassist, Mel Schacher, came from a certain cartoon character once upon a time - "Nobody knows the band Grand Funk? The wild shirtless lyrics of Mark Farner? The bong-rattling bass of Mel Schacher? The competent drumwork of Don Brewer? *Oh, man!*" Yep, I think Homer Simpson just about nailed what was so special about Mel when he had a bass in his hands during the late '60s/early '70s.

And he was the architect of one of the greatest bass tones known throughout all mankind - of course, I'm talking about Grand Funk's killer self-titled sophomore offering (aka *The Red Album*) just before the close of the 1960's. To sample this titanic tone, don't walk, *run* to such tracks as "Paranoid" (not to be confused with the B. Sabbath ditty of the same name) and "Inside Looking Out."

Standouts: "I'm Your Captain/Closer to Home," "Some Kind of Wonderful," "Inside Looking Out," "Paranoid," "Into the Sun"

Similar: Dennis Dunaway, Felix Pappalardi, Geezer Butler, Roger Glover, Rushton Moreve

Instruments: Gibson Ripper, Fender Jazz, Fender Precision, Zon Sonus 4

Pick or Fingers: Pick

55.
Dennis Dunaway
(Alice Cooper)

Story: With theatrics and shock rock serving as the focal point of most of Alice Cooper's press coverage early on, some foolishly overlooked the fact that the band possessed an outstanding bass player in its ranks, Dennis Dunaway. What made Dunaway stand out from the rest of the early '70s rock bassist crop (an era which proved to be quite dense with countless standout musicians - Tim Bogert, Chris Squire, Geezer Butler, etc.) was he would utilize a drone/open string approach, as evidenced on such tunes as "Gutter Cat vs. the Jets."

And the beginning of "Unfinished Sweet" always reminded me of Cliff Burton for some reason (perhaps due to Dennis' use of a wah pedal)...although this would've been a full decade *before* Mr. Burton burst on the scene with Metallica. 'Tis a shame that the original Cooper band did not stick together longer - as once the band split in 1974, not much else was heard from Dunaway and his heavily-mirrored Fender Jazz and green n' sparkly Gibson EB-0 (the latter affectionately known as the "Frog Bass").

Standouts: "Is It My Body?", "Gutter Cat vs. the Jets," "Unfinished Sweet," "Blue Turk," "Generation Landslide"

Similar: Paul McCartney, Jack Bruce, Dave Alexander, Roger Glover, Gene Simmons

Instruments: Fender Jazz, Gibson EB-0

Pick or Fingers: Pick

54.
Bill Wyman
(The Rolling Stones)

Story: It would be tough to pick a winner in the highly-coveted "Bassist Who Most Resembled A Statue On Stage" competition between two British bass giants, John Entwistle and...Bill Wyman. Regardless, both certainly made up for their lack of on-stage enthusiasm with countless classic basslines and grooves.

In the case of Mr. Wyman (real name - William Perks Jr.), he could blend in with whatever style of song Jagger and Richards decided to take on - resulting in some quite memorable bass moments on such tunes as the disco-ish "Miss You," the funky "Undercover of the Night," and the arena rocker "Start Me Up." And you have to give props to Wyman for penning and singing lead on one of the oddest tunes ("In Another Land") from one of the oddest albums (*Their Satanic Majesties Request*) of the Stones' entire catalog.

Standouts: "Miss You," "Live With Me," "Under My Thumb," "Start Me Up," "Undercover of the Night"

Similar: Pete Quaife, Paul McCartney, Paul Samwell-Smith, Chas Chandler, Tom Hamilton

Instruments: Gibson EB-3, Ampeg Dan Armstrong, Bass Centre Wyman, Vox Teardrop, Steinberger XM2

Pick or Fingers: Pick

53.
Roger Waters
(Pink Floyd)

Story: Perhaps due to his immense talents as a songwriter, lyricist, and conceptualist (and also sharing the stage with one of rock's all-time great guitarists), the bass skills of Roger Waters are not necessarily one of the first things you think of concerning Pink Floyd. But upon closer inspection, he certainly has offered his share of classic basslines - tops being one of the most instantly recognizable bass bits ever, "Money."

And although Floyd is primarily pegged as a "prog band" by many, Mr. Waters could also get downright funky at times - especially on such *Wall* classics as "Run Like Hell," "Young Lust," and "Another Brick in the Wall, Part 2." And there is an unspoken rule that whenever a bassist is the main singer and songwriter of his or her band, they have automatically earned special bonus points in the eyes of fellow four-string pluckers/thumpers everywhere. So for that, Mr. Waters...we congratulate you!

Standouts: "Money," "Young Lust," "Hey You," "Run Like Hell," "Have a Cigar"

Similar: John Wetton, Greg Lake, Paul McCartney, Bill Wyman, John Paul Jones

Instruments: Fender Precision, Fender Jazz

Pick or Fingers: Pick

52.
Tim Commerford
(Rage Against the Machine, Audioslave, Prophets of Rage)

Story: I totally agree with you - rap metal is by and large an extremely stinky genre. But one of the few exceptions to this golden rule (the *only* exception?) was Rage Against the Machine. And the main reason why RATM has stood the test of time was how utterly brilliant the instrumentalists in the band were - including their awesomely tattooed bassist, Tim Commerford.

While there is no denying that he frequents the funk, it appears as though Tim's main bass role model was Rush's Geddy Lee - as evidenced by his penchant for playing Fender Jazz models and a *Moving Pictures*-esque tone at times. And with RATM ceasing to exist for large chunks,

Commerford has collaborated with a few of his mates in a pair of off-shoot bands - Audioslave (which featured the late/great Chris Cornell of Soundgarden on vocals) and Prophets of Rage (which features Chuck D of Public Enemy and B-Real of Cypress Hill).

Standouts: "Killing in the Name," "Bullet in the Head," "Bulls on Parade," "Township Rebellion," "Take the Power Back"

Similar: Geddy Lee, Fieldy, Robert Trujillo, Shavo Odadjian, Flea

Instruments: Fender Jazz, Music Man Sting Ray

Pick or Fingers: Fingers

51.
Justin Chancellor
(Tool)

Story: What are Tool? New age zen metal? Regardless of this puzzling problem, you have to give the band credit for coming up with a unique and original hard rock/heavy metal approach during the early '90s - an era which seemed like every other week there was a new/interesting band to discover (the polar opposite of today, eh?). And when it came time for Tool to replace their original bassist, Paul D'Amour, they could not have picked a better feller than Justin Chancellor.

Chancellor's style can be described as alternating between repetitive and rubbery (and even a bit percussive at times) - a fine example of "the repetitive" being "Schism," and "the rubbery" being the title track off their sophomore full-length, *Ænema*. And I will always have the utmost respect for señor Chancellor from a personal point of view - after some schlemiel nailed him in the neck/head region with a cup of beer during the first song of a Tool show that I attended (at the Continental Arena in New Jersey, on August 15, 2002), instead of storming off stage Axl-style, he simply continued on and played the full set, undeterred.

Standouts: "Ænema," "Schism," "The Grudge," "Forty Six & 2," "Jambi"

Similar: Paul D'Amour, Tony Levin, Dick Lövgren, Les Claypool, Paz Lenchantin

Instruments: Music Man Stingray, Wal 4-string fretless, Wal Mark III, Wal Mark II, Warwick Custom Shop Masterbuilt Streamer Stage II

Pick or Fingers: Pick

50.
Robert Trujillo
(Metallica, Ozzy Osbourne, Infectious Grooves, Suicidal Tendencies)

Story: Few rock/metal bassists have as impressive a résumé as Robert Trujillo. Don't believe me? The facts speak for themselves - Suicidal Tendencies, Infectious Grooves, Ozzy Osbourne, Jerry Cantrell, Glenn Tipton, Black Label Society, and Metallica have all enlisted Trujillo at various points. And while his two main areas of stylistic expertise are metal and funk, Trujillo certainly gets extra "good guy points" for co-writing and co-producing an outstanding documentary about Jaco Pastorius (2014's *Jaco*), which undoubtedly helped introduce the bass legend to a whole new generation of players.

And to the jealousy of bassists everywhere, Robert is now the proud owner of Jaco's iconic "Bass of Doom" instrument (a fretless 1962 Fender Jazz Bass - which has been refurbished - as evidenced by a scene in *Jaco,* where he is playing the instrument in concert with Metallica). We must give Trujillo even further credit for re-introducing the importance of *low-end* bass back into Metallica's sound upon his joining the band in 2003 (something that had been woefully muted upon the arrival of Jason Newsted). And lastly, his "crab walk" while performing on stage has become a crucial component of what we all hold so dear about the man known to his family as Roberto Agustín Miguel Santiago Samuel Perez de la Santa Concepción Trujillo Veracruz Batista.

Standouts: "Punk It Up" (Infectious Grooves), "Violent and Funky" (Infectious Grooves), "I Wasn't Meant to Feel This/Asleep at the Wheel" (Suicidal Tendencies), "Cyanide" (Metallica), "Spit Out the Bone" (Metallica)

Similar: Geezer Butler, Cliff Burton, Flea, Norwood Fisher, Les Claypool

Instruments: Fender Precision, Fender Jazz, Warwick Robert Trujillo Streamer Signature, Tobias Toby Deluxe V, Music Man Stingray

Pick or Fingers: Fingers

49.
Norwood Fisher
(Fishbone)

Story: Flea was not the only one slapping popping, and thumping his bass during the mid to late '80s (and fearlessly combining funk together with the punk). No siree. There was at least one other bassist who was part of the same alt rock underground scene as the Red Hot Chili Peppers, that was causing a buzz - *and doing it right.* Of course, I'm talking about Fishbone's John Norwood Fisher (best known as simply "Norwood Fisher").

Fisher's bass playing was obviously influenced by such '70s funk giants as Bootsy Collins and Verdine White. But by injecting his playing with the adrenaline surge of punk rock, Fisher's playing on such classic Fishbone releases as 1988's *Truth and Soul* is absolutely awe-inspiring - especially on the it-needs-to-be-heard-to-be-believed bass solo in the middle of "Bonin' in the Boneyard."

Standouts: "Bonin' in the Boneyard," "When Problems Arise," "Party at Ground Zero," "Freddie's Dead," "Everyday Sunshine"

Similar: Flea, Bootsy Collins, Billy "Bass" Nelson, Verdine White, Les Claypool

Instruments: Warwick CS Infinity, Fender Precision

Pick or Fingers: Fingers

48.
Billy "Bass" Nelson
(Parliament-Funkadelic)

Story: Although many automatically think of Bootsy Collins concerning the topic of "P-Funk bassists," the bass on Funkadelic's classic early recordings - including their greatest album in my humble opinion, 1971's *Maggot Brain* - was supplied by a chap by the name of Billy Nelson (also known as "Billy Bass"). The late/great guitarist Eddie Hazel seemed to be showcased the most during this harder rocking era of the band (especially on the gloriously Hendrix-y guitar-led instrumental title track from *Maggot Brain*). But Nelson's bass can certainly be felt/heard on a number of tracks - specifically a song he sings, "You and Your Folks, Me and My Folks." Additionally, Nelson's name was introduced to a whole new generation of bassists, when both Flea and Norwood Fisher sang his high praises in interviews circa the early '90s.

Standouts: "You and Your Folks, Me and My Folks," "Wars of Armageddon," "Back In Our Minds," "Music for My Mother," "Better By the Pound"

Similar: Flea, Norwood Fisher, Billy Cox, Rusty Allen, George Porter Jr.

Instruments: Fender Precision

Pick or Fingers: Fingers

47.
Verdine White
(Earth, Wind and Fire)

Story: Few bands can get a dancefloor shaking as mightily as Earth, Wind and Fire - especially when they were in the midst of issuing their string of classic hits in the '70s. And it was bassist Verdine White who provided many a funk groove - "Shining Star," "Serpentine Fire," "Got to Get You Into My Life," etc. In addition to his superb abilities on the four-string (be sure to search out his bass solo at the massive California Jam Festival from 1974 - it is YouTube-able), you also have to respect Verdine's skills as a levitationist (a gimmick he utilized back in the good old days at EW&F concerts).

Standouts: "Shining Star," "Serpentine Fire," "That's the Way of the World," "Can't Hide Love," "Got to Get You Into My Life"

Similar: Bernard Edwards, Bootsy Collins, Larry Graham, Marshall "Rock" Jones, Rick James

Instruments: Sadowsky Verdine White Signature, Warwick Streamer LX, Ibanez VWB1, Yamaha BB3000, Fender Aerodyne Jazz

Pick or Fingers: Fingers

46.
Muzz Skillings
(Living Colour)

Story: When you're the bassist in a band with musicians who are impressively at the top of their game as Living Colour, it would be understandable to have difficulty holding your own. But LC's original bassist, Muzz Skillings, had no complications at all - offering up first-rate funky and groove-heavy bass parts throughout their two most popular (and possibly, best) albums, 1988's *Vivid* and 1990's *Time's Up.*

Playing ESP basses at the time (LC guitarist Vernon Reid was also an "ESP man" early on, before moving on to Hamer), Skillings' talents are most exemplified on his solo smack dab in the middle of the ballad, "Broken Hearts," as well as his slap-happy/funk-heavy "Funny Vibe," and the experimental bass showcase, "Ology." Unfortunately, after exiting LC in 1992, not much has been heard from this extremely talented player.

Standouts: "Funny Vibe," "Ology," "Time's Up," "Broken Hearts," "What's Your Favorite Color?"

Similar: Darryl Jenifer, Flea, Rick Skatore, Doug Wimbish, Robert Trujillo

Instruments: Custom ESP 4

Pick or Fingers: Fingers

45.

Doug Wimbish
(Living Colour)

Story: Doug Wimbish had some mighty big shoes to fill when he was asked to replace Muzz Skillings in Living Colour. But with a résumé that already included serving as part of the rhythm section on classic recordings for Sugarhill Records - including supplying the awesome bassline on "White Lines (Don't Do It)" by Grandmaster & Melle Mel - as well as the experimental funk act Tackhead, LC couldn't have picked a better chap. And the "new look" line-up certainly delivered on their highly underrated 1993 album, *Stain.*

What sets Wimbish apart from most rock bassists is that rather than plucking the strings with this right hand in a traditional manner, he usually either slaps or taps his lines, while never being afraid to plug into a wide variety of effects. Doug has remained in the bass position with Living Colour ever since (save for a band hiatus from 1995-2000), and has also guested on recordings by the Rolling Stones, Depeche Mode, and Joe Satriani, among others.

Standouts: "Go Away" (Living Colour), "Leave It Alone" (Living Colour), "Nothingness" (Living Colour), "WTFF" (Living Colour), "White Lines (Don't Do It)" (Grandmaster & Melle Mel)

Similar: Muzz Skillings, Tim Commerford, Les Claypool, Norwood Fisher, Thundercat

Instruments: Spector Euro 4 LX Doug Wimbish Signature

Pick or Fingers: Fingers

44.

Greg Lake
(ELP, King Crimson)

Story: If only one human being could be awarded "the world's first prog rock bassist," Greg Lake would quite possibly be most deserving of this cherished title. The reason? Bloody hell, he was the singer/bassist on classic recordings by both King Crimson *and* Emerson, Lake and Palmer! And it turned out that Lake knew his way around an acoustic guitar, as well ("Still You Turn Me On") and even knew a thing or two about penning a holiday classic ("I Believe in Father Christmas"). But to truly behold the majestic might of Lake's bludgeoning bass, be sure to hunt down on YouTube the stark "bass track" or "bass and drums track" of Crimson's "21st Century Schizoid Man," and forward to the middle part. Your earholes are guaranteed to be flabbergasted at the rapid-fire bass play.

Standouts: "21st Century Schizoid Man" (King Crimson), "In the Court of the Crimson King" (King Crimson), "Bullfrog" (ELP), "From the Beginning" (ELP), "Karn Evil 9: 2nd Impression" (ELP)

Similar: Chris Squire, John Wetton, Jeffrey Hammond, Mike Rutherford, Roger Waters

Instruments: Fender Jazz, Fender Precision, Wal MK II, Zemaitis Double Neck, Alembic Scorpion 8-string, Rickenbacker 4001

Pick or Fingers: Pick

43.
John Wetton
(King Crimson, UK, Asia)

Story: When most pop fans first discovered John Wetton during the early '80s (1982 to be precise - with the runaway chart success of Asia's self-titled debut, and the hit single "Heat of the Moment"), it was undoubtedly his fine singing voice that was the main focus. But long-time prog-heads knew the truth - he was also an exceptional bassist. Serving as a key member of the heaviest era of King Crimson (they managed to be even blacker than Sabbath in the year 1974, with *Red*), Wetton was also a part of one of the trickiest prog bands ever, UK (1978's self-titled debut confirms this bold claim).

Additionally, Wetton was a highly-sought "hired gun" by other acts, including time spent supplying the low-end for Roxy Music, Uriah Heep, and Wishbone Ash. And lastly, Wetton gets my vote for creating one of the best bass tones on record during the early '70s - throughout the aforementioned *Red* recording.

Standouts: "The Great Deceiver" (King Crimson), "Red" (King Crimson), "Starless" (King Crimson), "In the Dead of Night" (UK), "Danger Money" (UK)

Similar: Greg Lake, Chris Squire, Boz Burrell, Mike Rutherford, Bob Daisley

Instruments: Fender Precision, Gibson Victory Standard, Zon Legacy "Il Gato Negro"

Pick or Fingers: Pick

42.
Glenn Cornick
(Jethro Tull)

Story: While most rockers could *not* pull off the headband look, Jethro Tull's original bassist, Glenn Cornick, was one of the lucky few that *did* manage to pull of this typically treacherous task. As Tull's bassist during what some (including I) consider their classic period of 1967-1970, Cornick often played the "lead bassist" role in the band, especially on the exceptional instrumental, "Bourée," as well as the bouncy bossa nova feel of "Living in the Past."

And Cornick's presence in the band must have kept Tull leader Ian Anderson in check, because shortly after the bassist was handed his walking papers, the band began embarking on entire album side-long (some say "indulgent") compositions, before ultimately, losing the plot. Sadly, any chance of a reunion of the *Stand Up/Benefit* Tull line-up was nullified in 2014, when Cornick passed away, at the age of 67.

Standouts: "Living in the Past," "Bourée," "Nothing Is Easy," "A Song for Jeffrey," "Jeffrey Goes to Leicester Square"

Similar: John Paul Jones, Jack Bruce, John Entwistle, Geezer Butler, Noel Redding

Instruments: Gibson EB-2, Gibson EB-3, Gibson Thunderbird, Fender Jazz

Pick or Fingers: Fingers

41.
Phil Chen
(Jeff Beck, Rod Stewart)

Story: Throughout the course of rock history, there have been very few notable bassists who are of Chinese ancestry, by way of Kingston, Jamaica. But Phil Chen is one of the few who can stake this claim. And he just so happened to have been in the right place at the right time - namely, inside AIR Studios in London, circa October 1974, when Jeff

Beck was working on his landmark instrumental/jazz-fusion masterpiece, *Blow by Blow*.

Chen's penchant for funky bass was all over the *BbB* album (particularly the exquisite "Freeway Jam"), which certainly added some extra pizzazz to an already extraordinary collection of tunes. But Chen's most-heard bass playing was as a member of Rod Stewart's band circa the late '70s - particularly on the bawdy rocker "Hot Legs" and the disco smash "Da Ya Think I'm Sexy."

Standouts: "Freeway Jam" (Jeff Beck), "You Know What I Mean" (Jeff Beck), "Air Blower" (Jeff Beck), "Hot Legs" (Rod Stewart), "Da Ya Think I'm Sexy" (Rod Stewart)

Similar: James Jamerson, Donald "Duck" Dunn, Wilbur Bascomb, Bootsy Collins, Bernard Edwards

Instruments: Fender Precision

Pick or Fingers: Fingers

40.
Wilbur Bascomb
(Jeff Beck, James Brown)

Story: Perhaps the most underrated bassist in this entire bleeding book is a gentleman by the name of Wilbur Bascomb. While Wilbur's name may not ring any bells for many, the landmark album that his funky bass playing is featured throughout will - I'm talking about Jeff Beck's tour de force, *Wired. Blow by Blow* seems to get the lion's share of attention when it comes to Beck's top recordings, but little old me actually prefers *Wired* - an album that is much more "in your face," rocking, and *extremely* bass heavy (the opening of "Head for Backstage Pass" is an absolute must-hear for bassists).

And it turns out that Wilbur (man, I *love* saying that name - hopefully it makes a comeback real soon) also appeared on recordings by other artists, including George Benson and James Brown. And concerning the latter, I have read conflicting reports regarding if it is he or another bassist playing on the James Brown album, *Reality,* so I'm just going to hope for the best and include "Funky President" below as a standout. But despite his outstanding handle of the four-string, Bascomb never matched the ferocity and inspired playing detected throughout *Wired.*

Standouts: "Head for Backstage Pass" (Jeff Beck), "Led Boots" (Jeff Beck), "Come Dancing" (Jeff Beck), "Sophie" (Jeff Beck), "Funky President (People It's Bad)" (James Brown)

Similar: Stanley Clarke, Verdine White, Jaco Pastorius, Bootsy Collins, TM Stevens

Instruments: Fender Precision

Pick or Fingers: Fingers

39.
Thundercat

Story: During the early 21st century, it became maddeningly frustrating how many musicians seemed frightened about taking on a variety of styles - or even attempting to play with other artists from other genres. Thank heavens that Thundercat (real name - Stephen Bruner) came to the rescue just in the nick of time. As of this book's writing, the 33-year-old T-cat has already constructed an incredibly impressive and varied résumé - having played/recorded with the likes of Erykah Badu, Suicidal Tendencies, Kendrick Lamar, and Young Jazz Giants, among others.

But best of all are his solo albums - 2011's *The Golden Age of Apocalypse,* 2013's *Apocalypse,* and especially, 2017's *Drunk* - where his smooth-yet-funky basslines are the driving force (although admittedly sometimes drenched in Moog-y effects) behind such great tunes as "Them Changes" and the sublime "Show You the Way" (the latter of which features Michael McDonald and Kenny Loggins on vocals). And any bassist that can handle a monster six-string instrument while courageously wearing shorts, black socks, and white sandals (as he did during a performance on *The Tonight Show Starring Jimmy Fallon*) is a-OK in my book...literally.

Standouts: "Them Changes," "Show You the Way," "A Fan's Mail (Tron Song Suite II)," "Oh Sheit It's X," "Return to the Journey"

Similar: Stanley Clarke, Bootsy Collins, John Patitucci, Leonard "Hub" Hubbard, Squarepusher

Instruments: Ibanez Thundercat Signature 6-string

Pick or Fingers: Fingers

38.
Victor Wooten
(Béla Fleck and the Flecktones)

Story: The '90s seemed to be largely devoid of new bass guitar heroes…except for the emergence of Victor Wooten. First coming up as part of Béla Fleck and the Flecktones, it was around the time Wooten emerged as a solo artist (1996's *A Show of Hands*), that fans of electric bass began to take note en masse. Appealing to fans of both jam bands (due to his affiliation with Fleck) and jazz (Jaco Pastorius is an obvious influence, as evidenced by his fondness for harmonics), Wooten also ventures outside these genres.

Case in point, Wooten being enlisted by one of the most over-the-top heavy metal/guitar shred acts ever, Nitro, to handle bass duties on the group's reunion album (still to be titled/released upon this book's release). But perhaps to truly grasp the talents of Wooten, be sure to view one of his many unaccompanied bass solos on YouTube - which will serve as a virtual 101 course on tapping, slapping, popping, and proper harmonic placement on the bass.

Standouts: "U Can't Hold No Groove" (Victor Wooten), "Classical Thump" (Victor Wooten), "Sex in a Pan" (Béla Fleck and the Flecktones), "Funky D" (Wooten Chambers Franceschini), "Victa" (Victor Wooten)

Similar: Stu Hamm, Stefan Lessard, Jeff Berlin, Marcus Miller, Jaco Pastorius

Instruments: Fodera Yin Yang, Fodera Monarch, Compito Fretless 5

Pick or Fingers: Fingers

37.
Leigh Gorman
(Bow Wow Wow)

Story: One of the biggest "rock n' roll shames" was that most people could not look beyond the Mohawk haircuts of certain Bow Wow Wow members, and not see the terrific talents each member possessed - especially bassist Leigh Gorman. I'd be as bold to say that Gorman may have been the funkiest bass player within the pop realm circa the early '80s (perhaps only challenged by Duran Duran's John Taylor) - as heard/seen on the massive MTV hit, "I Want Candy."

But if you're not familiar with BWW or Gorman beyond that one ditty, by all means, dig a bit deeper (any old greatest hits comp will do), and you will discover one of the most underrated rock bassists ever. And by the late '80s, Gorman had obviously served as an inspiration for two of rock's top bass talents - Flea of the Red Hot Chili Peppers and Les Claypool of Primus.

Standouts: "I Want Candy," "Baby, Oh No," "Cowboy," "Do You Want to Hold Me?", "Go Wild in the Country"

Similar: John Taylor, Nick Beggs, Kevin Mooney, Flea, Les Claypool

Instruments: Wal Pro II

Pick or Fingers: Both

36.
Graham Maby
(Joe Jackson)

Story: When punk rock burst on the scene like an unapologetic brick through a window in the mid '70s, musicianship was frowned upon...especially when it came to bass playing - with most bassists playing with a pick and merely following the guitar concerning what to play. However, by the time the punk off-shoot genre, new wave, began to rear its head near the close of the decade, the value of musicianship was re-introduced to the proceedings. Case in point, Joe Jackson's long-time bassist, Graham Maby.

A good example of a bassist who knows when to make his presence felt/heard and when to take a backseat, Maby's bass certainly helped lead the charge on countless early Jackson classics - specifically the material on his first three albums, 1979's *Look Sharp!* and *I'm the Man,* plus 1980's *Beat Crazy.* And when the original JJ Band imploded after *BC,* Mr. Jackson retained a single member of the group for countless subsequent albums (including the singer/pianist's most commercially successful album, 1982's *Night and Day*) and tours. I'll let you take a wild guess who that lucky gentleman was...

Standouts: "Got the Time," "Look Sharp!", "Is She Really Going Out with Him?", "Mad at You," "Biology"

Similar: Bruce Foxton, Bruce Thomas, Colin Mouding, Peter Hook, John Taylor

Instruments: Fender Jazz, Spector NS-5

Pick or Fingers: Both

35.
Mark King
(Level 42)

Story: You can probably get away with the following statement - "The funkiest pop bassists to emerge out of the UK during the 1980's were Duran Duran's John Taylor, Bow Wow Wow's Leigh Gorman, and Level 42's Mark King" (I guess I just *did* get away with that statement, eh?). And in addition to being quite adept at slapping and popping his strings, King also possesses a fine singing voice, as well as a gift for penning a pop smash - as demonstrated by Level 42's biggest global hits, "Something About You' and "Lessons in Love."

And you've got to admire him even further for playing a

space-age looking bass - the Status Graphite KingBass Paramatrix - which is not only headless a la a Steinberger, but also, sports snazzy LED dots on the fretboard…which will come in quite handy the next time you're either trying to attract UFO's or directing a nighttime airplane landing.

Standouts: "Lessons in Love," "Something About You," "The Sun Goes Down," "Chinese Way," "The Chant Has Begun"

Similar: John Taylor, Leigh Gorman, Nick Beggs, Jeff Berlin, Stanley Clarke

Instruments: Status Graphite KingBass Paramatrix, Status The KingBass Mk II, Jaydee Supernatural

Pick or Fingers: Fingers

34.
Stu Hamm
(Joe Satriani, Steve Vai)

Story: Steve Vai certainly has a knack for attracting musicians that are exceptionally talented - especially early in his career. Case in point, being instructed by Joe Satriani, then while attending Berklee School of Music, crossing paths with two renowned bassists - Randy Coven and…Stu Hamm. First appearing on Vai's classic solo debut, *Flex-Able,* it was through their friendship that Hamm was introduced to Satriani, which lead to Satch/Stu touring together in support of the landmark *Surfing with the Alien* recording.

Also at the time, Hamm began issuing his own solo albums (1988's *Radio Free Albemuth,* 1989's *Kings of Sleep,* 1991's *The Urge,* etc.), which expectedly, put the main focus on the bass. Playing Kubicki Ex Factor basses, Hamm was slapping and popping before Flea popularized it within rock circa the late '80s/early '90s, and was fretboard tapping right alongside Billy Sheehan (which served as the basis for one of his best-known numbers - an unaccompanied bass rendition of "Linus and Lucy" from *Peanuts*). While he still performs/records, Hamm also shares his knowledge with other players - including serving as "Director of Bass Programs" at Musician's Institute in California...and was one of the few bassists lucky to be interviewed for my 2017 book, *Shredders!*

Standouts: "Quahogs Anyone?" [includes "Linus and Lucy"] (Stu Hamm), "Black Ice" (Stu Hamm), "Viv Woman" (Steve Vai), "Attitude Song" (Steve Vai), "The Bells of Lal (Part Two)" (Joe Satriani)

Similar: Billy Sheehan, Randy Coven, Dave LaRue, Jeff Berlin, Stanley Clarke

Instruments: Kubicki Ex Factor, Warwick Stu Hamm Signature, Fender Urge II, Washburn Stu Hamm Signature

Pick or Fingers: Fingers

33.
Jeff Berlin

Story: What the heck was it about the '70s and the '80s, where it seemed like almost every month (week? day?) there was a new amazingly-gifted-bassist to discover? Certainly, one of the top bassists to emerge during this era was Jeff Berlin, whose funky-yet-clean tone/approach served as an inspiration for subsequent players (most obvious being Stu Hamm).

Early on, Berlin seemed to be mostly associated with prog rock vets (including Yes alumni Patrick Moraz and Bill Bruford). But as the years went on, his name became most linked with jazz-fusion - particularly on solo recordings, including one of his best, 1986's *Pump It!* - and has even jammed with six-string shredders (namely Frank Gambale and Richie Kotzen) and shared the stage with Billy Sheehan and Hamm, as part of the BX3 Tour.

Standouts: "Joe Frazier" (Jeff Berlin), "Palewell Park" (Bill Bruford), "Gothic 17" (Bill Bruford), "Fainting in Coils" (Bill Bruford), "Tears in Heaven" (Jeff Berlin), "Freight Train Shuffle" (Jeff Berlin)

Similar: Jaco Pastorius, Stanley Clarke, Stu Hamm, Marcus Miller, Victor Wooten

Instruments: Cort Rithimic Jeff Berlin Signature, Peavey Palaedium (Jeff Berlin Signature), Dean USA Jeff Berlin Basic Signature Series

Pick or Fingers: Fingers

32.

Lemmy
(Motörhead, Hawkwind)

Story: Although certain rock bassists had been utilizing distortion as part of their sound since the '60s (Blue Cheer's Dickie Peterson was one of the earliest culprits), you can certainly make a valid case that it was not until Motörhead's Lemmy (real name - Ian Kilmister) arrived that it became popularized and properly "trademarked." First coming to the attention of the rock music underground as a member of space rockers Hawkwind (who scored a hit with a tune sung by Lemmy, "Silver Machine"), it was a blessing in disguise when he was ousted from the band after a drug bust - as it led to the formation of the mighty Motörhead.

With Lemmy now fully in control, the band specialized in an oft-copied style that merged punk and metal (and you could say even elements of vintage rock n' roll). And it was Lemmy's distorted and loud bass sound (by playing his trusty Rickenbacker 4001 through Marshall amplification) that proved to be a major ingredient in his band's sound - as heard on such all-time headbanger classics as "Ace of Spades" and "Overkill."

Standouts: "Ace of Spades," "Overkill," "Stone Dead Forever," "Motörhead," "Iron Fist"

Similar: Cliff Burton, Jimmy Bain, Enid Williams, Steve Dawson, Dickie Peterson

Instruments: Rickenbacker 4001

Pick or Fingers: Pick

31.
John Myung
(Dream Theater)

Story: I don't care what you say - by the late '80s, prog rock was pretty much dead (I know...*except* for Rush). However, a style of music known as "prog metal" was starting to sprout, as evidenced by such popular albums as *...And Justice for All* by Metallica and *Operation: Mindcrime* by Queensrÿche, and especially, with the emergence of Dream Theater. And as you may have guessed, every single bloody member of the band was outstanding on their instrument - including bassist John Myung. Throughout the rock and metal landscape, there are only a select few bassists I would confidently say can play any tricky bit of music you throw their way. But I'd feel mighty confident placing my trust in Mr. Myung's capabilities.

Standouts: "The Ytse Jam," "Metropolis, Pt. 1: The Miracle and The Sleeper," "Panic Attack," "The Dance of Eternity," "Take the Time"

Similar: Geddy Lee, Steve Harris, Wally Voss, Billy Sheehan, Dave LaRue

Instruments: Music Man Bongo 6, Music Man Bongo 5, Ernie Ball Music Man Stingray, Yamaha RBX6 JM2, Spector (unsure of model)

Pick or Fingers: Fingers

30.

John Deacon
(Queen)

Story: Although not the flashiest bassist to ever strap on the instrument, John Deacon's contribution to what made Queen so mighty cannot be understated. Despite opting to blend into the background (especially on stage), it was Deacon's songwriting that proved to be an essential ingredient ("Another One Bites the Dust," "You're My Best Friend"), as well as composing some of the most instantly-recognizable basslines in rock history (the aforementioned "Another One Bites the Dust," plus "Under Pressure").

Some overlooked Queen tunes contain some fine and fluid bass solos from Deacon, including the beginning of "The Millionaire Waltz" and just before the guitar solo in "Breakthru." But perhaps his best bass playing can be sampled on the funk-rocker "Dragon Attack," which contains a killer riff, and one of Deacon's best bass solos (again, right before Brian May's guitar solo kicks in).

Standouts: "Dragon Attack," "Another One Bites the Dust," "Under Pressure," "The Millionaire Waltz," "Breakthru"

Similar: Paul McCartney, Bill Wyman, John Paul Jones, Sting, Adam Clayton

Instruments: Fender Precision, Music Man Stingray, Kramer DMZ 4001

Pick or Fingers: Both

29.
Aston Barrett
(Bob Marley and the Wailers)

Story: If you could only choose one bassist who truly embodies reggae, Aston Barrett - who provided bass on Bob Marley's classic recordings - would most definitely be a deserving recipient. After all, it is Aston's bass that you hear on one of Bob Marley's most renowned songs (make that one of *reggae's* most renowned songs), "Is This Love."

With his spacious basslines and grooves, Barrett proved to be incredibly influential - not only on other up-and-coming reggae bassists (such as Sly and Robbie's Robbie Shakespeare, but also on plenty of punk rock and new wave bassists, as well (the Clash's Paul Simonon, the Bad Brains' Darryl Jenifer, the Police's Sting, etc.). And in addition to his timeless work with Marley, Barrett has lent his bass talents to other artists, including Marley's son, Ziggy, plus

Peter Tosh and Lee "Scratch" Perry, among others.

Standouts: "Is This Love" (Bob Marley) "One Drop" (Bob Marley), "Africa Unite" (Bob Marley), "Zimbabwe" (Bob Marley), "X Marks the Spot" (Ziggy Marley)

Similar: Robbie Shakespeare, Sting, Darryl Jenifer, Aaron "P-Nut" Wills, Tony Kanal

Instruments: Fender Jazz, ESP LTD B-1006

Pick or Fingers: Fingers

28.
John Taylor
(Duran Duran, Power Station)

Story: Some couldn't get past how gosh darn good-looking Duran Duran was. But unlike most pop teeny bop bands of the past, the members of the group were talented instrumentalists, and also, deserve kudos for penning their hits without the aid of outside songsmiths. From about 1982-1986, if you were to view MTV for any extended period of time, chances are you would definitely spot a video clip from DD, or from one of its off-shoot groups. And of all the pop groups championed by the station at the time, John Taylor was one of - if not *the* - top bassists.

For many (and admittedly, yours truly), it was after the fact concerning this realization - especially the basslines on such hits as "Rio," "Planet Earth," and "Girls on Film." Also,

Taylor has the distinction of being in one of the few off-shoot groups of a popular band that did *not* suck. Of course, I am referring to the Power Station, and their bass-heavy hit, "Some Like It Hot."

Standouts: "Rio" (Duran Duran), "Hungry Like the Wolf" (Duran Duran), "Planet Earth" (Duran Duran), "Some Like It Hot" (Power Station), "Girls on Film" (Duran Duran)

Similar: Leigh Gorman, Bernard Edwards, Nick Beggs, Mick Karn, Mikey Craig

Instruments: Aria Pro II SB-1000, Aria Pro II SB-1000JT, Kubicki Ex Factor

Pick or Fingers: Fingers

27.
Tina Weymouth
(Talking Heads, Tom Tom Club)

Story: Not very many funky bassists came out of the original CBGB's scene in NYC circa the mid to late '70s (which was known primarily for punk rock). But the Talking Heads' Tina Weymouth was certainly a notable exception. And when I say "funky," I don't mean of the Verdine White/Bootsy Collins variety (in other words, lotsa slappin' and poppin').

Weymouth's specialty was creating bass grooves that quite often served as a lead instrument (while both David Byrne and Jerry Harrison were great rhythm guitar players, they very rarely dared to attempt a guitar solo - leaving it to such professionals as Adrian Belew on stage). Case in point, such TH hits as "Psycho Killer" and "Once in a Lifetime," the lesser-known "Stay Hungry" and "Cities," and we mustn't forget the hit single "Genius of Love" by the TH off-shoot group, the Tom Tom Club, either.

Standouts: "Once in a Lifetime," "Psycho Killer," "Take Me to the River," "Crosseyed and Painless," "Warning Sign"

Similar: Jah Wobble, Graham Maby, Adam Clayton, Busta "Cherry" Jones, Sara Lee

Instruments: Hofner Club, Fender Mustang, Gibson Les Paul Triumph, Veillette-Citron Standard

Pick or Fingers: Both

26.
Billy Cox
(Jimi Hendrix, Band of Gypsys)

Story: Musicians and eventual bandmates usually meet each other in a variety of different ways - classified ads, performing as part of the same local music scene, through mutual acquaintances, etc. *The Army* is not exactly tops on the list of meeting like-minded musicians. But that is exactly what happened to Billy Cox and Jimi Hendrix circa 1961, when both first crossed paths - and began playing music together shortly thereafter - while stationed in Fort Campbell, Kentucky.

After successfully tracking Cox down after hitting the big time with the Jimi Hendrix Experience, the two immediately formed a new band, Band of Gypsys, which as evidenced by their lone self-titled recording, leaned heavy on the jammier side of things (but features some killer grooves, especially on "Changes"). Cox was set to continue on with Jimi beyond the Gypsys, as he was working on what was to be Hendrix's next studio album, *First Rays of the New Rising Sun* (which featured more succinct songwriting), before Hendrix's tragic death extinguished the promising Jimi-Billy reunion.

Standouts: "Who Knows," "Machine Gun," "Changes," "Night Bird Flying," "In From the Storm"

Similar: James Jamerson, Donald "Duck" Dunn, John Paul Jones, Berry Oakley, Tommy Shannon

Instruments: Fender Precision, Fender Jazz

Pick or Fingers: Fingers

25.
Noel Redding
(The Jimi Hendrix Experience)

Story: Make no bones about it - when you're in a band with Jimi Hendrix, you *will* get overlooked. But to Noel Redding's credit, he did find a way to fit exceptional bass into some of rock's all-time great compositions, as a member of the Jimi Hendrix Experience. A guitarist-turned-bassist, Redding quite often utilized his bass as a lead instrument, as if he was doing battle with Jimi for the spotlight (a simply blazing rendition of "Killing Floor" off *Live at Monterey* is a prime example).

But perhaps what kept the late Redding from obtaining "bass God" status was two-fold. Firstly, Jimi was known to handle bass chores himself in the studio from time to time (including one of the JHE's most bass-featured tracks, "1983"), and secondly, Noel seemed to turn his attentions to another band, Fat Mattress, that was not nearly as good as the Experience - contributing to the JHE's split in 1969.

Standouts: "Killing Floor," "Third Stone from the Sun," "Castles Made of Sand," "If 6 Was 9," "She's So Fine"

Similar: Jack Bruce, Mel Schacher, Tim Bogert, Roger Glover, Phil Lynott

Instruments: Fender Jazz, Gibson EB-2, Hagstrom 8-string

Pick or Fingers: Pick

24.

Tim Bogert
(Vanilla Fudge, Cactus, Beck Bogert Appice)

Story: If I could award only a pair of bassists who helped trailblaze the fine art of "lead bass" within the realm of rock n' roll, I'd feel very confident selecting both John Entwistle and Tim Bogert (well…probably Jack Bruce too, but let's just focus on the first two for the moment, shall we?). While Entwistle has received his rightful amount of praise over the years (obviously due to the immense popularity of the Who), Bogert seems to be often overlooked. Which is unfortunate - he was simply one helluva bassist (both from the standpoint of what his fingers could do on the fretboard, and also, his massive tone).

Although probably best known as a member of proto-metallists Vanilla Fudge, it was his work with the underrated Cactus and the frustratingly short-lived Beck Bogert Appice where he truly showed off his bass aptitude. With a tone similar to Mel Schacher of Grand Funk, Bogert simply kicks ass on such juicy prime cuts as Cactus' "Guiltless Glider" and BBA's "Lady," and has been name-checked as a prime influence by quite a few renowned bassists, namely Billy Sheehan (who modeled his infamous bass, "The Wife," after Bogert's Fender P-Bass with a Tele neck).

Standouts: "You Keep Me Hanging On" (Vanilla Fudge), "You Can't Judge A Book By the Cover" (Cactus),

"Guiltless Glider" (Cactus), "Lady" (Beck Bogert Appice), "Superstition" (Beck Bogert Appice)

Similar: John Entwistle, Mel Schacher, John Paul Jones, Michael Anthony, Billy Sheehan

Instruments: Fender Precision (with Telecaster neck), Michael Tobias Design 6-string, Fodera Tim Bogert Signature 6-string

Pick or Fingers: Fingers

23.
Bernard Edwards
(Chic)

Story: Bass proved crucial to disco artists of the '70s - as it certainly equated to getting rumps a-shaking on the dance floor. And quite a few basslines by the late/great Bernard Edwards of Chic undoubtedly caused a commotion at Studio 54 back in the day. Seemingly, every single Chic song has an outstanding bassline serving as its foundation - case in point, "Good Times," "Le Freak," and especially, the jaw-droppingly brilliant "Everybody Dance." And the bassline to "Good Times" inspired other artists, as evidenced by very similar grooves being heard shortly afterwards in "Rapper's Delight" by the Sugarhill Gang and "Another One Bites the Dust" by Queen. Undoubtedly, one of the greatest funk/dance bassists of all-time.

Standouts: "Good Times," "Le Freak," "Everybody Dance," "I Want Your Love," "Chic Cheer"

Similar: Bootsy Collins, Larry Graham, Louis Johnson, Rick James, Robert "Kool" Bell

Instruments: Fender Precision, Music Man Stingray, BC Rich Eagle

Pick or Fingers: Fingers

22.
Mike Watt
(The Minutemen, fIREHOSE, The Stooges)

Story: While it is tempting to neatly say "the first bassist to merge punk and funk together was Flea," this just isn't the case, dear readers. A chap by the name of Mike Watt just may have been the first - as heard in his work with the Minutemen during the early/mid '80s, and later, as a member of fIREHOSE and as a solo artist (while a stint with Iggy & the Stooges erased the "funk" part of the equation).

While Watt's penchant for basslines that wander in and out of key may upset some traditional 4-string sticklers, he has indeed come up with his own unique/instantly recognizable playing style, as heard in such tunes as "Corona" (best known as the theme song for the *Jackass* film/TV franchise) and "Down with the Bass." And Watt's scruffy appearance (he has been "bearded" of varying lengths, sported well-worn flannel shirts, jeans, and Converse sneakers) and his speak/sing vocal style only adds to his charm.

Standouts: "Down with the Bass" (fIREHOSE), "Corona" (The Minutemen), "Big Train" (Mike Watt), "Epoxy, for Example" (fIREHOSE), "This Ain't No Picnic" (The Minutemen)

Similar: Flea, Cris Kirkwood, Les Claypool, Martyn LeNoble, Richard Hell

Instruments: Reverend Wattplower, Gibson EB-3, Fender Precision, Gibson Thunderbird, Gibson Les Paul Signature

Pick or Fingers: Both (but mostly fingers)

21.
John Paul Jones
(Led Zeppelin)

Story: To think, if Jimmy Page did not invite John Paul Jones (real name - John Richard Baldwin) to join his then-fledgling band, the New Yardbirds, the bassist may have spent the rest of his life toiling away as a faceless session musician. Luckily, he accepted, and soon after, the New Yardbirds was rechristened Led Zeppelin and...we all know the rest of the story.

Similar to a Rush or Queen situation - where all the members of the band are outstanding on their respective instrument - Jones' work with Zeppelin covered a wide variety of styles. And no matter what Jones was called upon to do in the bass department, he had no problem adapting (proto-metal, blues, funk, folk, country, prog, etc.). Also, you have to give Jones additional props for when after his Zeppelin days were done in 1980, he went on to either produce and/or play with a variety of different artists, including Diamanda Galas, the Butthole Surfers, and Them Crooked Vultures, among others.

Standouts: "The Lemon Song," "Heartbreaker," "The Crunge," "Dazed and Confused," "Whole Lotta Love"

Similar: James Jamerson, Carol Kaye, Paul McCartney, Tim Bogert, John Deacon

Instruments: Fender Jazz, Alembic Series II, Alembic 8-string, Manson E-Bass John Paul Jones Signature Bass Guitar

Pick or Fingers: Both (but mostly fingers)

20.
Geezer Butler
(Black Sabbath)

Story: Similar to Noel Redding, Black Sabbath's Geezer Butler was a transplanted six-stringer to four-stringer. But unlike Noel, Geezer (real name - Terry Butler) is considered one of the first-ever genuine heavy metal bassists, helping lay down the groundwork for the big riffs and high volume that would run rampant throughout the '70s and beyond.

Most impressive is that Butler found a way to shine alongside one of metal's all-time great riff meisters, guitarist Tony Iommi, whose dense n' detuned n' plodding riffing didn't leave a whole heck of a lotta space for ol' Geezer to thump away. But as heard on such all-time metal classics as "NIB," "Iron Man," and "War Pigs," he somehow found a way to make already heavy riffs even, um, *heavier.*

Standouts: "Bassically/NIB," "Heaven and Hell," "War Pigs," "Iron Man," "Planet Caravan"

Similar: Jack Bruce, Dennis Dunaway, Cliff Burton, Ben Shepherd, Andrew Weiss

Instruments: Fender Precision, BC Rich Eagle, Vigier Passion 5, Lakland Geezer Butler Signature

Pick or Fingers: Fingers

19.
Sting
(The Police)

Story: The Police's Sting (real name - Gordon Sumner) was a perfect example of how a minimalist bass style could help serve the song...while also somehow managing to show off that he was one heck of a bassist, in the process. One of rock's more underrated instrumentalists (I guess since he was also the singer and songwriter of countless hit songs obscured that fact), Sting originally came from a jazz background - before undergoing a "reggae-punk makeover" in time for the Police's debut album, *Outlandos d'Amour,* in 1978.

Perhaps no greater example of Sting's gift for composing simple basslines that served as the backbone of a song is on "Walking on the Moon," while on tunes such as "Spirits in the Material World," he shows impressive finger flash on the fretboard. And Sting gets extra added bonus points for being one of the few pop artists of the '80s bold enough to utilize upright bass (spotted in their most popular single/video - "Every Breath You Take"), as well as managing to name-check both author Vladimir Nabokov and the mythological sea creatures Scylla and Charybdis in hit songs ("Don't Stand So Close to Me" and "Wrapped Around Your Finger," respectively).

Standouts: "Walking on the Moon," "Masoko Tanga," "Regatta De Blanc," "Spirits in the Material World," "Can't Stand Losing You"

Similar: Graham Maby, Tina Weymouth, John Taylor, Leigh Gorman, Aston Barrett

Instruments: Fender Precision, Spector NS2, Steinberger L2, Ibanez MC-940 Fretless, Hamer 8-string Fretless, Van Zalinge Z Bass Electric Upright

Pick or Fingers: Both

18.

Donald "Duck" Dunn
(Booker T & the MG's,
The Blues Brothers)

Story: Just think - if it wasn't for the classic 1980 comedy film, *The Blues Brothers,* many would not have known who the heck Donald "Duck" Dunn was. But this was certainly not because of his instrumental prowess - as a member of soul greats Booker T & the MG's, Dunn provided outstanding bass grooves on not just classic tracks by the band (which were all-instrumental), but also backing other artists, as BT&TMG's doubled as Stax Records' house band. As a result, Dunn (who replaced original Booker bassist Lewie Steinberg in the band) can be heard on classic recordings by the likes of Otis Redding ("Sittin' on the Dock of the Bay"), Sam & Dave ("Hold On, I'm Comin'"), and Albert King ("Born Under a Bad Sign"). And while it is *not* Dunn playing bass on BT&TMG's best known tune, "Green Onions" (that is Steinberg), he did appear on other classics by the group, including "Time is Tight," "Hip Hug-Her," and "Hang 'Em High," among others.

Dunn (who supposedly got his famous nickname from his father, from watching Disney cartoons, and specifically, those starring Donald Duck) also played with a variety of legendary artists during his lifetime, including Muddy Waters, Eric Clapton, and Neil Young. But it was as a member of the soul revival act, the Blues Brothers (fronted by actors/singers John Belushi and Dan Aykroyd) that Dunn received his most publicity - due to his appearance in the aforementioned movie, and offering the classic line, *"We had a band powerful enough to turn goat piss into gasoline."*

Standouts: "Time is Tight" (Booker T & the MG's), "Hip Hug-Her" (Booker T & the MG's), "Hold On, I'm Comin'" (Sam & Dave), "Born Under a Bad Sign" (Albert King), "(Sittin' on the) Dock of the Bay" (Otis Redding)

Similar: James Jamerson, Lewie Steinberg, Carol Kaye, John Paul Jones, Jack Bruce

Instruments: Fender Precision, Fender Duck Dunn Precision, Lakland Duck Dunn Signature

Pick or Fingers: Fingers

17.
Carol Kaye

Story: If you listen to classic pop hits from the '60s and '70s for any lengthy duration, you are most certain to - unknowingly - hear a bassline provided by Carol Kaye. Beginning work as a session musician (her first session was recordings for Sam Cooke), Kaye eventually became part of the Wrecking Crew - a group of Los Angeles-based session musicians that played on countless recordings by major artists, as well as being considered the "go-to band" for producer Phil Spector.

Being able to adapt her bass playing to a variety of styles (and also playing other instruments, as well), Kaye's basslines have appeared on countless classic recordings. Case in point, albums by the Beach Boys (*Pet Sounds*), Neil Young (his self-titled debut), and Frank Zappa (*Freak Out!* and *Absolutely Free*), as well as such hit singles as Glen Campbell's "Rhinestone Cowboy," the Monkees' "I'm a Believer," and Barbra Streisand's "The Way We Were," among others.

Standouts: "These Boots Are Made for Walkin'" (Nancy Sinatra), "Feelin' Alright" (Joe Cocker), "Sloop John B" (Beach Boys), "A Natural Man" (Lou Rawls), "Wichita Lineman" (Glen Campbell)

Similar: James Jamerson, John Paul Jones, Donald "Duck" Dunn, Paul McCartney, Jack Bruce

Instruments: Fender Precision, Ibanez SRX-690, Music Man Stingray

Pick or Fingers: Both

16.
James Jamerson

Story: James Jamerson was probably the most *heard* soul/R&B bassist of all-time. And the reason why is simple - he served as a session musician for Motown Records during their golden era (the '60s and '70s), as a member of a collective known as the Funk Brothers. In the process, Jamerson played on countless classic recordings, including hits by Marvin Gaye, the Jackson 5, Stevie Wonder, the Supremes, Gladys Knight, and the Four Tops, among many others.

You could even make the argument that it may have been Jamerson who helped create what we all know and love nowadays as "funk," as his basslines had a distinguishable groove and bounce to them - which obviously served as an influence on such subsequent celebrated funk players as Larry Graham and Bootsy Collins. Unfortunately, Jamerson's name is not as well-known as it should be to casual music fans, as Motown at the time did not properly credit the session musicians on their recordings (and he passed away in 1983, long before the internet made it easier to look up which musicians played on what). Regardless, many of Jamerson's bass grooves remain legendary.

Standouts: "Inner City Blues (Make Me Wanna Holler)" (Marvin Gaye), "What's Going On" (Marvin Gaye), "Ain't No Mountain High Enough" (Marvin Gaye and Tammi Terrell), "It's The Same Old Song" (Four Tops), "Bernadette" (Four Tops)

Similar: Carol Kaye, Donald "Duck" Dunn, Lewie Steinberg, Wilton Felder, Bernard Odum

Instruments: Fender Precision

Pick or Fingers: Fingers

15.

Cliff Burton
(Metallica)

Story: Cliff Burton was thrash metal's first true bass hero. And what made him stand out from the rest of the pack during the early to mid '80s was while seemingly every hard rock/heavy metal bassist was squeezing into spandex and primping their hair, Mr. Burton was a throwback to the '70s - donning well-worn bell bottom jeans, a denim jacket, and long (yet hairsprayed-less) hair. But that was just from a "looks" standpoint. From a musical standpoint, he was even *more* unique. Playing with his fingers (again, in a sub-genre of metal in which the majority of bassists play with a pick) and utilizing distortion and a wah pedal as part of his sound, Burton offered a different angle on rock bass playing at the time.

More influenced by the likes of Lynyrd Skynyrd than Iron Maiden, Burton's bass talents were prominently on display on such Metallica classics as "(Anesthesia) - Pulling Teeth" (half of which is an unaccompanied bass solo), "Orion" (which features a four-string creating some very "un-bass like" sounds, and harmonies), as well as "For Whom the Bell Tolls" (which begins with lead bass). Tragically, one of metal's most promising musicians died in a freakish bus crash while on tour in support of Metallica's breakthrough album, *Master of Puppets*, on September 27, 1986, at the age of 24 (and has subsequently been replaced by Jason Newsted, and then Robert Trujillo). But if we are to be perfectly honest, the three albums that Burton plays on (*Kill*

'Em All, Ride the Lightning, and *Master of Puppets*) are unquestionably Metallica's best - which confirms how essential Burton was to the band.

Standouts: "(Anesthesia) - Pulling Teeth," "Orion," "For Whom the Bell Tolls," "The Call of Ktulu," "Damage, Inc."

Similar: Geezer Butler, Geddy Lee, Lemmy, Andrew Weiss, Robert Trujillo

Instruments: Aria Pro II SB-1000, Rickenbacker 4001, Alembic Spoiler

Pick or Fingers: Fingers

14.

Flea
(Red Hot Chili Peppers)

Story: A valid argument could be made that it was not until the Red Hot Chili Peppers' Flea (real name - Michael Balzary) burst onto the scene in the mid-late '80s that the slap bass technique was finally fully accepted within rock music. Up to this point, slapping and popping was assigned almost exclusively to funk and dance styles. But with the group's commercial breakthrough (namely 1989's *Mother's Milk* and 1991's *Blood Sugar Sex Magik*), "punk funk" was introduced to the world, and did an absolutely swell job of merging both aforementioned styles together.

And to his credit, after seemingly every single rock bassist was suddenly exploring the slap technique circa 1990/1991, Flea made a conscious decision to put the brakes on it for the *BSSM* album. But still, was able to offer up basslines that helped boost many of the album's tracks. Case in point, one of the Chili Peppers' most popular and enduring tunes, "Give It Away." The Peppers may have gone on to embrace more commercial sounds (a move that certainly paid off from a chart success standpoint), but we will always have such splendid early classics like *The Uplift Mofo Party Plan* to be reminded of when the Chili Peppers were truly red hot.

Standouts: "Get Up and Jump," "Fight Like a Brave," "Higher Ground," "Give It Away," "Pretty Little Ditty"

Similar: Norwood Fisher, Robert Trujillo, Les Claypool, Bootsy Collins, Billy "Bass" Nelson

Instruments: Music Man Stingray 5, Modulus Flea Bass, Fender Flea Signature Jazz Bass

Pick or Fingers: Fingers

13.
Bootsy Collins
(James Brown,
Parliament-Funkadelic,
Bootsy's Rubber Band)

Story: If there was ever a "bass superhero," Bootsy Collins would certainly be the right man for the job. Beginning with his affiliation with Parliament-Funkadelic in the early '70s, the always-superbly attired/sunglass-sporting Bootsy (real name - William Collins) has been spotted slapping and thumping a star-shaped instrument - that goes by the name of "Space Bass" - ever since.

On tracks by P-Funk ("Mothership Connection") and Bootsy's Rubber Band ("Bootzilla"), he certainly "brings the bass." However, it was his marvelous earlier work with James Brown - including a track that I would vote for as the #1 funk tune of all-time, "Get Up (I Feel Like Being a) Sex Machine" - that shows why many consider Bootsy to be one of the all-time bass greats.

Standouts: "Get Up (I Feel Like Being a) Sex Machine" (James Brown), "Super Bad" (James Brown), "Soul Power" (James Brown), "Mothership Connection (Star Child)" (Parliament), "Bootzilla" (Bootsy's Rubber Band)

Similar: Cordell Boogie Mosson, Billy "Bass" Nelson, James Jamerson, George Porter Jr., Flea

Instruments: Fender Jazz, Warwick Bootsy Collins Infinity Signature, Warwick Bootsy Collins Spacebass, Washburn Custom Shop Bootsy Collins Limited Edition Space Bass

Pick or Fingers: Fingers

12.

Jack Bruce
(Cream)

Story: When you have crafted one of the greatest riffs of all-time, you're destined for greatness and immortality amongst musicians. And Jack Bruce certainly achieved both. Best known for his magnificent work with Cream, it was with this band (rock's first-ever power trio, by the way) that he gave us the hypnotic riff that I just alluded to - "Sunshine of Your Love." Along with "Smoke on the Water" and "Iron Man," "SoYL" has become one of rock's most instantly recognizable riffs, as well as one of the first that just about any guitarist-to-be initially learns on their instrument (and has also proven to be a popular tune in films, as evidenced by its riff sneaking its way into key scenes in both *The Breakfast Club* and *Goodfellas*).

Coming from a jazz background, it was upon uniting with singer/guitarist Eric Clapton and drummer Ginger Baker in Cream circa 1966 that Bruce (who was the top singer in the group, by the way) carved his niche on a global scale. And after Cream's dissolution in 1968, Bruce embarked on a solo career (including penning/recording the classic tune "Theme for an Imaginary Western," which Mountain popularized), and briefly uniting with Mountain's Leslie West and Corky Laing in West, Bruce and Laing (whose underrated debut, 1972's *Why Dontcha,* was quite Cream-like), as well as playing with others (Vernon Reid, Phil Manzanera, etc.), before passing away on October 25, 2014, at the age of 71.

Standouts: "Crossroads," "Sunshine of Your Love," "Badge," "White Room," "Anyone for Tennis"

Similar: John Paul Jones, Tim Bogert, Felix Pappalardi, Glenn Cornick, Jaco Pastorius

Instruments: Fender VI, Gibson EB-3, Warwick Jack Bruce Limited Edition Fretless Thumb, Warwick Jack Bruce JB3 Signature Survivor, Warwick Jack Bruce Thumb NT

Pick or Fingers: Fingers

11.
Tony Levin
(King Crimson, Peter Gabriel)

Story: As a session musician, it is mostly your job to blend in and not stand out all that much. And Tony Levin did as he was told while playing on sessions for such legendary artists as John Lennon, Alice Cooper, Pink Floyd, David Bowie, and Tom Waits. But as a full-on member of King Crimson and as a long-time studio/touring member of Peter Gabriel's band, he was allowed to run buck wild. And run buck wild he did - with often glorious results.

Spotted playing either a traditional four-string instrument, a Chapman Stick, or an upright, Levin's playing tends to be both funky and percussive (he even created something called "Funk Fingers," which are akin to drumsticks…but for the bass) - but not to the detriment of the song. And absolutely nothing sounded like the opening to KC's "Elephant Talk" until Mr. Levin came along (and was a clear precursor to Les Claypool's playing style - specifically on Primus' "Jerry Was a Race Car Driver").

Standouts: "Elephant Talk" (King Crimson), "Thela Hun Ginjeet" (King Crimson), "Shock the Monkey" (Peter Gabriel), "Sleepless" (King Crimson), "Indiscipline" (King Crimson)

Similar: Les Claypool, Trey Gunn, Gail Ann Dorsey, Stu Hamm, Doug Wimbish

Instruments: Music Man Stingray, Chapman Stick

Pick or Fingers: Fingers

10.
Paul McCartney
(The Beatles, Wings)

Story: I would venture to guess that the rock bassist that inspired the most musicians to pick up the four-string would have to be the Beatles' Paul McCartney. Countless artists over the years have pinpointed the Fab Four's first-ever appearance on *The Ed Sullivan Show* on February 9, 1964 as a defining moment in their decision to pursue music, while those born after the fact were attracted solely by hearing the music. Now that we've gotten that out of the way, McCartney (who plays his bass left-handed) was probably the most technically-gifted musician of the band, as his basslines certainly helped propel such tunes as "Rain," "Taxman," and "Paperback Writer."

Additionally, McCartney's gift for coming up with basslines that provided support - while not getting in the way of the band's trademark vocal harmonies and melodies - is certainly remarkable ("Michelle," "Something," "Hey Jude," etc.). And of course, the fact that he was one half of the greatest rock songwriting duo of all-time solidifies Sir Paul's standing as one of the top bassists in this book (if you have to ask who the other half was...I'm going to politely decline being the person who informs you).

Standouts: "Come Together," "Rain," "Taxman," "I Want You (She's So Heavy)," "Paperback Writer"

Similar: Bill Wyman, Roger Waters, John Entwistle, John Paul Jones, Brian Wilson

Instruments: Höfner 500/1, Rickenbacker 4001, Wal MK2 5-string, Yamaha BB 1200

Pick or Fingers: Both

9.
Steve Harris
(Iron Maiden)

Story: Before Steve Harris, the word "galloping" was not often used to describe a bassline. But upon hearing his unparalleled playing on such Iron Maiden classics as "The

Trooper," it is almost impossible to not picture...a horse trotting along! In addition to his special bass skills, Harris also gets extra credit for being the undisputed leader of the group (he's the only original member still in attendance) *and* their main songwriter.

Also, Harris introduced flatwound bass strings to the world of heavy metal - which admittedly, can be a bit of a double-edged sword (as his "clackity clack" bass sound can be a distraction at times - listen to the live recording *Maiden England* to hear what I'm talking about). However, Harris' contributions within the realm of heavy metal bass cannot be understated, and was probably only second to Billy Sheehan concerning who was the greatest hard rock/heavy metal bassist to emerge in the '80s.

Standouts: "The Trooper," "Wrathchild," "Innocent Exile," "Losfer Words (Big 'Orra)," "Phantom of the Opera"

Similar: John Entwistle, Geezer Butler, Billy Sheehan, Frank Bello, John Myung

Instruments: Fender Precision

Pick or Fingers: Fingers

8.
Larry Graham
(Sly and the Family Stone, Graham Central Station)

Story: Slapping, thumping, and popping the bass guitar swept soul and dance music in the '70s - a style that saw the instrument being played in a much more percussive manner than the traditional approach. And the inventor of this style? Mr. Larry Graham Jr. As a member of one of the most popular soul/pop bands of the late '60s/early '70s, Sly and the Family Stone, Graham's aforementioned ground-breaking technique (which he came up with while accompanying his piano-playing mother at church, and needed to provide the rhythm since there was no drummer) was prominently displayed on the massive hit singles "Everyday People" and - especially - "Thank You (Falettinme Be Mice Elf Agin)."

And once Graham exited Sly's band at seemingly the height of their popularity (1972), he didn't waste time launching his own outstanding band, Graham Central Station, which picked up right where his previous employer left off. In fact, it sounded as if Larry was now free to prominently display his bass talents even further on four-string showcases ("The Jam"), while also continuing to offer songs that, like Sly, contained commentary/observations about society ("Hair"). The funkiest bass player of all-time? Without question.

Standouts: "Thank You (Falettinme Be Mice Elf Agin)" (Sly & the Family Stone), "Sex Machine" (Sly & the Family Stone), "Hair" (Graham Central Station), "The Jam" (Graham Central Station), "Thank You for Talking to Me Africa" (Sly & the Family Stone)

Similar: Stanley Clarke, Verdine White, Bootsy Collins, Flea, Les Claypool

Instruments: Warwick Larry Graham Signature Bass Guitar, Moon JJ-4 300B, Vox Sidewinder, Fender Jazz

Pick or Fingers: Fingers

7.
Billy Sheehan
(David Lee Roth, Mr. Big, Sons of Apollo, Winery Dogs, Talas)

Story: Eddie Van Halen was the most covered and discussed rock guitarist in the music press throughout the '80s. And when it came to rock bass, Billy Sheehan was his counterpart. Similar to EVH, Sheehan employed the "two hand tapping technique" on the fretboard of his well-worn P-Bass with a Tele neck, which he dubbed "The Wife" (the jury is still out over who "tapped" first, as both Sheehan and EVH started doing it while playing clubs in the early '70s, albeit on their respective east and west coasts). And something else that both had in common was while they were both technically brilliant, they knew when not to overplay, and how to hold down the almighty rhythmic groove.

Starting out as a member of the somewhat faceless Buffalo rock band Talas, it wasn't until Sheehan scored a then-highly coveted gig - as the bassist for David Lee Roth (who was freshly out of Van Halen) - that he finally got the recognition he deserved. When teamed with fellow guitar wiz Steve Vai, the resulting album, 1986's *Eat 'Em and Smile,* was a massive hit, and did an excellent job of appealing to both rockers, pop listeners, and fellow musicians obsessed with shred-tastic playing. Although Sheehan's gig with Roth was frustratingly short-lived (lasting only two years), his career continued to thrive, as a member of such bands as Mr. Big, Winery Dogs, and Sons of Apollo.

Standouts: "Shyboy" (David Lee Roth and Talas), "Elephant Gun" (David Lee Roth), "Yankee Rose" (David Lee Roth), "NV43345" (Talas), "Addicted to That Rush" (Mr. Big)

Similar: John Entwistle, Tim Bogert, Stu Hamm, Randy Coven, Jeff Berlin

Instruments: Yamaha Attitude, Fender Precision (aka "The Wife")

Pick or Fingers: Fingers

6.
Chris Squire
(Yes)

Story: To some bass buffs, any player that dare play the instrument with a pick is frowned upon. But this opinion is hogwash. And I have all the proof you'll ever need - just listen to the extraordinary bass work of Yes' Chris Squire (who indeed utilized a plectrum throughout this career) for this old-school rule to be blasted to smithereens. Also, Mr. Squire wasn't afraid to add a little distortion to his bass sound - which was copied by quite a few subsequent bassists.

It's no secret that all of Yes' members were grossly talented on their respective instruments, and when called upon, Squire's basslines could lead the charge ("Heart of the Sunrise") or offer much-need support ("Owner of a Lonely Heart"). But if you were to select a single track that proves once and for all that bass guitar can be featured front and center and won't flounder, point your ears in the direction of Squire's wondrous bass showcase, "The Fish (Schindleria Praematurus)."

Standouts: "Long Distance Runaround/The Fish (Schindleria Praematurus)," "Heart of the Sunrise," "Roundabout," "Siberian Khatru," "Close to the Edge"

Similar: Geddy Lee, John Wetton, Greg Lake, John Entwistle, Les Claypool

Instruments: Rickenbacker 4001, Mouradian CS-74, Custom Triple Neck Wal

Pick or Fingers: Pick

5.
Stanley Clarke
(Return to Forever)

Story: If you want to see a jazz-fusion bassist break into a sweat, offer them the following question - "Which bassist trailblazed jazz-fusion more supremely - Stanley Clarke or Jaco Pastorius?" If it were up to me, I may take the easy way out and say it would be a two-way tie. But hey, this isn't Jaco's entry, this is Stanley's, so let's get back on track here! First bursting onto the scene with Return to Forever in 1972, it was on such subsequent fusion classics as 1973's *Hymn of the Seventh Galaxy,* 1974's *Where Have I Known You Before,* and 1975's *No Mystery* that Clarke's style - which mashed funk and jazz together - became solidified and identifiable.

But it was his solo recordings that truly captured the essence of Stanley's flexible yet durable bass playing - albums such as 1973's *Children Of Forever*, 1974's self-titled, 1975's *Journey To Love*, and 1976's *School Days* have understandably gone on to become iconic bass recordings. And it was also Clarke that helped popularize two bass makes that have subsequently become utilized by other players - Alembic and Carl Thompson.

Standouts: "School Days," "Vulcan Princess," "Lopsy Lu," "Silly Putty," "Hello Jeff"

Similar: Les Claypool, Leigh Gorman, Victor Wooten, Larry Graham, Tony Levin

Instruments: Alembic Stanley Clarke Signature, Gibson G3, Carl Thompson Piccolo

Pick or Fingers: Fingers

4.

Les Claypool
(Primus, Oysterhead, The Frog Brigade, Sausage, The Claypool Lennon Delirium)

Story: As mentioned earlier (Tim Commerford's entry, to be precise), there was an absolutely awful musical style that began stinking up the joint circa the late '80s/early '90s, known as funk metal. Thankfully, around the time, grunge altered the musical landscape, and this aforementioned foul-smelling style was flushed down the toilet. But there were several exceptions - most obviously, Primus. While the majority of other hard rock bands that injected funk into their sound at the time had probably only recently discovered the Red Hot Chili Peppers (and were suddenly trying to wedge Flea-style slapping/popping into their metal riffage), Primus' singer/bassist Les Claypool did not focus on the technical aspect of it. Rather, *rhythmic basslines* were his main focus.

Claypool's instrument of choice was the not-so-common Carl Thompson brand (his two main instruments being a four-string outfitted with a whammy bar, the other a fretless six-string), while his lyrics were often witty and humorous ("Tommy the Cat," "Wynona's Big Brown Beaver") and Primus' song structures could also be proudly off-the-wall ("Eleven," "Is It Luck?"). Additionally, Les was largely responsible - for better or worse - for popularizing six-string basses in the '90s, thanks to his tapping, thumping, and slapping on such alt-rock hits as the aforementioned "Tommy the Cat," plus "Jerry Was a Race Car Driver" and "My Name is Mud." The result was probably the most original-sounding rock bassist to emerge in the '90s. On second thought, make that one of the most original-sounding rock bassists *ever.*

Standouts: "Tommy the Cat," "Jerry Was a Race Car Driver," "My Name is Mud," "Those Damned Blue-Collar Tweekers," "John the Fisherman"

Similar: Tony Levin, Geddy Lee, Stanley Clarke, Leigh Gorman, Flea

Instruments: Carl Thompson 4-string, Carl Thompson fretless 6-string (aka "The Rainbow Bass"), Pachyderm

Pick or Fingers: Fingers

3.
Geddy Lee
(Rush)

Story: Few bassists in the history of rock have been as universally loved/admired across the board as Rush's Geddy Lee (real name - Gary Weinrib). Picture Yes' Chris Squire playing with his fingers rather than a pick, while also leaning more towards the harder rocking side of things, and you'd sorta be close to understanding Mr. Lee's sound/style/approach. And during Rush's "glory period" (I'm talkin' 'bout 1976-1982), few rock bassists were able to capture a tone on record as superbly as Mr. Lee - listen to the entire bloody *Moving Pictures* album for the sonic proof.

And in addition to all his outstanding bass work, Lee also found a way to multi-task - not only providing lead vocals in the band, but also, supplying keyboards and even stomping on synthesizer foot pedals...all the while having to navigate through some very treacherous/dangerous song structures! But Lee managed to come out of it not only unharmed, but also managed to thrive - resulting in being listed as a prime influence on some of rock's all-time great bassists, including Metallica's Cliff Burton and Primus' Les Claypool, among many others.

Standouts: "YYZ," "Digital Man," "Tom Sawyer," "Xanadu," "Analog Kid"

Similar: John Entwistle, Chris Squire, Billy Sheehan, Cliff Burton, Les Claypool

Instruments: Fender Jazz, Fender Precision, Rickenbacker 4001, Wal MK II, Steinberger L2

Pick or Fingers: Fingers

2.

Jaco Pastorius
(Weather Report, Joni Mitchell)

Story: Look up "bass guitar legend" in the music dictionary (is there really such an entry?), and a photo of Jaco Pastorius would simply have to be included. As evidenced by his outstanding work as a solo artist, a member of Weather Report, and on a string of albums by Joni Mitchell (as well as appearances on recordings by others), there was never a bassist as effortlessly funky *and* jazzy as John Francis Anthony "Jaco" Pastorius III. And I'll be so bold as to declare that it was Jaco who popularized fretless electric bass, and also, the use of harmonics (concerning the latter, prior to such Pastorius classics as "Portrait of Tracy," harmonics were used merely to tune a bass…not to base *an entire song* around).

Along with Stanley Clarke, Pastorius helped trailblaze jazz-fusion for bassists worldwide. For the proof that backs up this bold statement, just listen to virtually any selection off of Weather Report's *Heavy Weather* or Jaco's self-titled solo release (and put it in perspective by remembering what mainstream music sounded like during the mid '70s), and you're guaranteed to have your socks knocked off. And lastly, a friendly disclaimer - since Jaco was not a pure rock bassist, I reserved the top spot in this book for a player who was. But if this book was about simply the 100 greatest *bassists,* admittedly, Pastorius could have very well been numero uno.

Standouts: "Portrait of Tracy" (Jaco Pastorius), "Donna Lee" (Jaco Pastorius), "The Chicken" (Jaco Pastorius), "The Dry Cleaner from Des Moines" (Joni Mitchell), "Punk Jazz" (Weather Report)

Similar: Charles Mingus, James Jamerson, Stanley Clarke, Marcus Miller, John Patitucci

Instruments: Fender Jazz (aka "The Bass of Doom")

Pick or Fingers: Fingers

1.
John Entwistle
(The Who)

Story: The Who's John Entwistle was rock music's first honest-to-goodness "bass hero." After all, up to this point, most rock bassists merely held down the bottom and followed the guitarist's lead. But not Mr. Entwistle - a man affectionately known by two nicknames, "Thunderfingers" and "The Ox." Perhaps making up for the fact that the Who's guitarist, Pete Townshend, wasn't much of a lead player (but a helluva rhythm player and songwriter), Entwistle's fleet-fingered basslines helped fill up any empty spaces in such classic tunes as "My Generation" - which featured *a bass solo* rather than *a guitar solo.*

And besides providing massive basslines and grooves (with the treble cranked up high...and often the distortion, too), he was technically-gifted, to boot - specializing in a tapping technique that also employed harmonics, and sounded like no other rock bass player at the time. Or ever since, on second thought. Additionally, Entwistle gets bonus points for playing an awesome-looking instrument - shaped like a certain dastardly bird. So, at this point, I would like to congratulate the late/great John Entwistle for being #1 in my book...literally!

Standouts: "My Generation," "Boris the Spider," "The Real Me," "Won't Get Fooled Again," "Sister Disco"

Similar: Billy Sheehan, Steve Harris, Chris Squire, Noel Redding, Paul McCartney

Instruments: Modulus Graphite Buzzard, Warwick Buzzard, Fender Precision, Gibson Thunderbird, Alembic Series I, Alembic Explorer

Pick or Fingers: Both (but mostly fingers…hence his nickname, Thunderfingers!)

Complete List

101. Derek Smalls (Spinal Tap)
100. Richard Hell (Richard Hell and the Voidoids)
99. Glen Matlock (Sex Pistols)
98. Dee Dee Ramone (The Ramones)
97. Paul Simonon (The Clash)
96. Mark Evans & Cliff Williams (AC/DC)
95. Colin Greenwood (Radiohead)
94. Jesse F. Keeler (Death from Above)
93. Doug Pinnick (King's X)
92. Tom Petersson (Cheap Trick)
91. Klaus Flouride (Dead Kennedys)
90. Bruce Foxton (The Jam)
89. Bruce Thomas (Elvis Costello and the Attractions)
88. Robert Sledge (Ben Folds Five)
87. Ben Shepherd (Soundgarden)
86. Mark Sandman (Morphine)
85. Krist Novoselic (Nirvana)
84. Andrew Weiss (Rollins Band, Ween, Gone)
83. Peter Hook (Joy Division, New Order)
82. Jah Wobble (Public Image Limited, Jah Wobble's Invaders of the Heart)
81. Martyn LeNoble (Porno for Pyros)
80. Bob Daisley (Ozzy Osbourne, Rainbow)
79. Glenn Hughes (Deep Purple, Trapeze, Black Country Communion)
78. Michael Anthony (Van Halen, Chickenfoot)
77. Brian Wilson (The Beach Boys)
76. Phil Lesh (Grateful Dead)
75. Tommy Shannon (Stevie Ray Vaughan and Double Trouble, Johnny Winter)
74. Herbie Flowers (Lou Reed, David Bowie)
73. Trevor Bolder (David Bowie and the Spiders from Mars, Uriah Heep)
72. Trevor Dunn (Mr. Bungle, Fantômas)

71. Frank Bello (Anthrax)
70. Dan Lilker (Stormtroopers of Death, Nuclear Assault, Brutal Truth, Anthrax)
69. David Ellefson (Megadeth)
68. Joey DeMaio (Manowar)
67. Randy Coven
66. Darryl Jenifer (Bad Brains)
65. Cris Kirkwood (Meat Puppets)
64. Jeff Ament (Pearl Jam, Temple of the Dog, Mother Love Bone)
63. Eric Avery (Jane's Addiction)
62. Bill Gould (Faith No More)
61. Dave Allen (Gang of Four)
60. Adam Clayton (U2)
59. Phil Lynott (Thin Lizzy)
58. Gene Simmons (Kiss)
57. Roger Glover (Deep Purple, Rainbow)
56. Mel Schacher (Grand Funk)
55. Dennis Dunaway (Alice Cooper)
54. Bill Wyman (The Rolling Stones)
53. Roger Waters (Pink Floyd)
52. Tim Commerford (Rage Against the Machine, Audioslave, Prophets of Rage)
51. Justin Chancellor (Tool)
50. Robert Trujillo (Metallica, Ozzy Osbourne, Infectious Grooves, Suicidal Tendencies)
49. Norwood Fisher (Fishbone)
48. Billy "Bass" Nelson (Parliament-Funkadelic)
47. Verdine White (Earth, Wind and Fire)
46. Muzz Skillings (Living Colour)
45. Doug Wimbish (Living Colour)
44. Greg Lake (ELP, King Crimson)
43. John Wetton (King Crimson, UK, Asia)
42. Glenn Cornick (Jethro Tull)

41. Phil Chen (Jeff Beck, Rod Stewart)
40. Wilbur Bascomb (Jeff Beck, James Brown)
39. Thundercat
38. Victor Wooten (Béla Fleck and the Flecktones)
37. Leigh Gorman (Bow Wow Wow)
36. Graham Maby (Joe Jackson)
35. Mark King (Level 42)
34. Stu Hamm (Joe Satriani, Steve Vai)
33. Jeff Berlin
32. Lemmy (Motörhead, Hawkwind)
31. John Myung (Dream Theater)
30. John Deacon (Queen)
29. Aston Barrett (Bob Marley and the Wailers)
28. John Taylor (Duran Duran, Power Station)
27. Tina Weymouth (Talking Heads, Tom Tom Club)
26. Billy Cox (Jimi Hendrix, Band of Gypsys)
25. Noel Redding (The Jimi Hendrix Experience)
24. Tim Bogert (Vanilla Fudge, Cactus, Beck Bogert Appice)
23. Bernard Edwards (Chic)
22. Mike Watt (The Minutemen, fIREHOSE, The Stooges)
21. John Paul Jones (Led Zeppelin)
20. Geezer Butler (Black Sabbath)
19. Sting (The Police)
18. Donald "Duck" Dunn (Booker T & the MG's, The Blues Brothers)
17. Carol Kaye
16. James Jamerson
15. Cliff Burton (Metallica)
14. Flea (Red Hot Chili Peppers)
13. Bootsy Collins (James Brown, Parliament-Funkadelic, Bootsy's Rubber Band)
12. Jack Bruce (Cream)

11. Tony Levin (King Crimson, Peter Gabriel)

10. Paul McCartney (The Beatles, Wings)

9. Steve Harris (Iron Maiden)

8. Larry Graham (Sly and the Family Stone, Graham Central Station)

7. Billy Sheehan (David Lee Roth, Mr. Big, Sons of Apollo, Winery Dogs, Talas)

6. Chris Squire (Yes)

5. Stanley Clarke (Return to Forever)

4. Les Claypool (Primus, Oysterhead, The Frog Brigade, Sausage, The Claypool Lennon Delirium)

3. Geddy Lee (Rush)

2. Jaco Pastorius (Weather Report, Joni Mitchell)

1. John Entwistle (The Who)

Honorable Mentions
(in alphabetical order!)

Jarkko Aaltonen (Korpiklaani)
Kenny Aaronson (Dust, Hagar Schon Aaronson Shriever)
Barry Adamson (Magazine, Nick Cave and the Bad Seeds)
Juan Alderete (Racer X, the Mars Volta)
Dave Alexander (The Stooges)
Tom Araya (Slayer)
Ron Asheton (The Stooges)
Melissa Auf der Maur (Hole, Smashing Pumpkins)
Pat Badger (Extreme)
Victor Bailey (Weather Report)
Jimmy Bain (Rainbow, Dio)
Chris Ballew (The Presidents of the United States of America)
Peter Baltes (Accept)
Paul Barker (The Blackouts, Ministry, Revolting Cocks)
Lou Barlow (Dinosaur Jr., Sebadoh)
Walter Becker (Steely Dan)
Nick Beggs (Kajagoogoo, Steve Hackett)
Robert "Kool" Bell (Kool & the Gang)
John Bentley (Squeeze)
Guy Berryman (Coldplay)
Matt Bissonette (David Lee Roth, Ringo Starr, Elton John)
Lori "Lorax" Black (The Melvins)
Tom Blankenship (My Morning Jacket)
Joe Bouchard (Blue Öyster Cult)
Dan K. Brown (The Fixx)
David Brown (Santana)
Mark "Brownmark" Brown (Prince and the Revolution)
Rex Brown (Pantera, Down)
Francis Buchholz (The Scorpions, Michael Schenker's Temple of Rock)
Jean-Jacques Burnel (The Stranglers)
Boz Burrell (King Crimson, Bad Company)
Tony Butler (Big Country)

John Cale (The Velvet Underground)
Jack Casady (Jefferson Airplane, Hot Tuna)
Gerald Casale (Devo)
Peter Cetera (Chicago)
Clive Chaman (Jeff Beck Group)
Chas Chandler (The Animals)
Chi Cheng (Deftones)
Greg Christian (Testament)
Mario Cipollina (Huey Lewis and the News)
Johnny Colt (The Black Crowes)
Stu Cook (Creedence Clearwater Revival)
Billy Corgan (Smashing Pumpkins)
Peter "Mars" Cowling (Pat Travers)
Cronos (Venom)
Steve Currie (T. Rex)
Holger Czukay (Can)
Paul D'Amour (Tool)
Kurt Danielson (Tad)
Rick Danko (The Band)
Michael Davis (The MC5)
Steve Dawson (Saxon)
Kim Deal (The Pixies)
Mike Dean (Corrosion of Conformity)
Robert DeLeo (Stone Temple Pilots)
Paul Denman (Sade)
James Dewar (Robin Trower)
Steve Di Giorgio (Death, Autopsy, Control Denied)
Mike Dirnt (Green Day)
John Doe (X)
Gail Ann Dorsey (David Bowie)
Chris Dreja (The Yardbirds)
Steven Drozd (The Flaming Lips)
Chuck Dukowski (Black Flag)
Nathan East (Fourplay, Eric Clapton, Phil Collins, Toto)

Colin Edwin (Porcupine Tree)
Shane Embury (Napalm Death)
Howie Epstein (Tom Petty and the Heartbreakers)
Roy Estrada (Frank Zappa)
Fred Fairbrass (Right Said Fred)
Pete Farndon (The Pretenders)
Wilton Felder (The Crusaders)
Beaver Felton
Fieldy (Korn)
Harley Flanagan (The Cro-Mags)
Andy Fletcher (Depeche Mode)
Mike Flores (Origin)
Mo Foster
Tom Fowler (Frank Zappa)
Jackie Fox (The Runaways)
Nikolai Fraiture (The Strokes)
Tony Franklin (The Firm, Blue Murder)
Andy Fraser (Free)
Matt Freeman (Rancid)
Simon Gallup (The Cure)
Maurice Gibb (The Bee Gees)
Melvin Gibbs (Rollins Band, Ronald Shannon Jackson and
the Decoding Society, Sonny Sharrock)
John Glascock (Jethro Tull)
Chris Glen (Michael Schenker Group, Sensational Alex
Harvey Band)
Kim Gordon (Sonic Youth)
Mike Gordon (Phish)
Rob Grange (Ted Nugent)
Paul Gray (Slipknot)
GC Green (Godflesh)
Mick Grøndahl (Jeff Buckley)
Trey Gunn (King Crimson)
Bruce Hall (REO Speedwagon)

Tom Hamilton (Aerosmith)
Jeffrey Hammond (Jethro Tull)
Buddy Hankerson (Slave)
Nigel Harrison (Blondie)
Jimmy Haslip (Yellowjackets)
Jonas Hellborg (John McLaughlin, Bill Laswell, Shawn Lane)
Dusty Hill (ZZ Top)
Ian Hill (Judas Priest)
Stuart Hill (Shudder to Think)
Josh Homme (Queens of the Stone Age)
Trevor Horn (The Buggles)
Leonard "Hub" Hubbard (The Roots)
John Illsley (Dire Straits)
Mike Inez (Alice in Chains, Ozzy Osbourne)
David J (Bauhaus, Love and Rockets)
Anthony Jackson (Al Di Meola, Lee Ritenour, Buddy Rich)
Eddie Jackson (Queensrÿche)
Jermaine Jackson (The Jacksons)
Paul Jackson (Herbie Hancock)
Randy Jackson (Journey)
Alex James (Blur)
Rick James
Prakash John (Alice Cooper, Lou Reed)
Alphonso Johnson (Weather Report, Santana)
Louis Johnson (The Brothers Johnson)
Busta "Cherry" Jones (Talking Heads, David Byrne)
Darryl Jones (Rolling Stones, Miles Davis, Sting)
Marshall "Rock" Jones (Ohio Players)
Percy Jones (Brand X)
Tony Kanal (No Doubt)
Arthur "Killer" Kane (New York Dolls)
Mick Karn (Japan)
Doug Keyser (Watchtower)

Bakithi Kumalo (Paul Simon)
Rick Laird (Mahavishnu Orchestra)
Ronnie Lane (The Faces)
Dave LaRue (Steve Morse Band, Dixie Dregs)
Bill Laswell
Jim Lea (Slade)
Sara Lee (Gang of Four)
Will Lee
Paz Lenchantin (A Perfect Circle, The Pixies)
Stefan Lessard (Dave Matthews Band)
Joe Lester (Intronaut)
Mike Levine (Triumph)
Dick Lövgren (Meshuggah)
Nick Lowe
Matt Lukin (Mudhoney, The Melvins)
Dan Maines (Clutch)
Sean Malone (Cynic)
Aimee Mann ('Til Tuesday)
Michael Manring (Michael Hedges)
Frank Maudsley (A Flock of Seagulls)
Reggie McBride (Stevie Wonder, Keb' Mo', Rod Stewart)
Duff McKagan (Guns N' Roses, Velvet Revolver)
John McVie (Fleetwood Mac)
Randy Meisner (Eagles, Poco)
Nate Mendel (Foo Fighters, Sunny Day Real Estate)
Martin Mendez (Opeth)
Mark "The Animal" Mendoza (Twisted Sister, The Dictators)
Mike Mesaros (The Smithereens)
Marcus Miller (Miles Davis, Herbie Hancock, Luther Vandross)
Mike Mills (REM)
Charles Mingus
Roy Mitchell-Cárdenas (Mutemath)

Cordell "Boogie" Mosson (Parliament-Funkadelic)
Colin Moulding (XTC)
Dee Murray (Elton John)
Meshell Ndegeocello
Jason Newsted (Metallica, Flotsam and Jetsam)
Prescott Niles (The Knack)
Greg Norton (Hüsker Dü)
Brian "Big Hands" O'Connor (Eagles of Death Metal)
Patrick O'Hearn (Frank Zappa, Missing Persons)
Nick O'Malley (Arctic Monkeys)
Berry Oakley (Allman Brothers)
Shavo Odadjian (System of a Down)
Bernard Odum (James Brown)
Mike Oldfield
Nick Oliveri (Queens of the Stone Age, Mondo Generator, The Dwarves)
Stefan Olsdal (Placebo)
Jerry Only (The Misfits)
Benjamin Orr (The Cars)
Shuggie Otis
P-Nut (311)
Richard Page (Mr. Mister)
Pino Palladino (The Who, Paul Young, Jeff Beck)
Bruce Palmer (Buffalo Springfield)
Chuck Panozzo (Styx)
Felix Pappalardi (Mountain)
Dave Parlatto (Frank Zappa)
Danny Partridge (The Partridge Family)
John Patitucci (Chick Corea, Wayne Shorter)
Jerry Peek (Steve Morse Band)
Dave Pegg (Fairport Convention, Jethro Tull)
Dickie Peterson (Blue Cheer)
Jeff Pilson (Dokken, Foreigner, Dio)
Jeff Pinkus (Butthole Surfers)

Paulo "Paulo Jr." Xisto Pinto Jr. (Sepultura)
Mike Porcaro (Toto)
George Porter Jr. (The Meters)
Tiran Porter (The Doobie Brothers)
Rocco Prestia (Tower of Power)
Steve Priest (Sweet)
Prince
Pete Quaife (The Kinks)
Suzi Quatro
Carl Radle (Derek and the Dominos, Eric Clapton)
Chuck Rainey
CJ Ramone (The Ramones)
Scott Reeder (The Obsessed, Fireball Ministry)
John Rees (Men at Work)
Greg Reeves (Crosby, Stills, Nash & Young)
Keanu Reeves (Dogstar)
John Regan (Ace Frehley, Peter Frampton)
Trent Reznor (Nine Inch Nails)
Greg Ridley (Humble Pie)
Brian Ritchie (Violent Femmes)
Ule Ritgen (Electric Sun)
Andy Roarke (The Smiths)
Lee Rocker (Stray Cats)
Kira Roessler (Black Flag, Dos)
Rick Rosas (Neil Young, Joe Walsh)
Andy Rourke (The Smiths)
Mike Rutherford (Genesis, Mike + the Mechanics)
Kevin Rutmanis (Tomahawk, Melvins)
Gary Ryan (Joan Jett & the Blackhearts)
Tony Sales (Iggy Pop, Tin Machine)
Troy Sanders (Mastodon, Killer Be Killed)
Paul Samwell-Smith (The Yardbirds)
Rudy Sarzo (Ozzy Osbourne, Quiet Riot, Whitesnake, Dio)
Fernando Saunders (Lou Reed)

Rick Savage (Def Leppard)
Jerry Scheff (Elvis Presley, the Doors)
Timothy B. Schmit (Eagles, Poco)
Joseph "Lucky" Scott (Curtis Mayfield)
Derf Scratch (Fear)
Captain Sensible (The Damned)
Matt Sharp (Weezer, the Rentals)
Eddie Shaw (The Monks)
Bobby Sheehan (Blues Traveler)
Fran Sheehan (Boston)
Stanley Sheldon (Peter Frampton, Tommy Bolin)
Burke Shelley (Budgie)
Billy Sherwood (Yes)
Scott Shriner (Weezer)
Michael Shuman (Queens of the Stone Age)
David Wm. Sims (Jesus Lizard)
Nikki Sixx (Mötley Crüe)
Rick Skatore (24-7 Spyz)
Lee Sklar
Brad Smith (Blind Melon, Abandon Jalopy)
Curt Smith (Tears for Fears)
Fred Smith (Television, Blondie)
Squarepusher
Mike Starr (Alice in Chains)
Peter Steele (Type O Negative, Carnivore)
Doug Stegmeyer (Billy Joel)
Lewie Steinberg (Booker T & the MG's.)
TM Stevens
Tommy Stinson (The Replacements, Guns N' Roses)
Daryl Stuermer (Genesis, Phil Collins)
Kasim Sulton (Utopia, Todd Rungren, Meat Loaf, Joan Jett)
Billy Talbot (Neil Young and Crazy Horse)
Gary Tallent (E Street Band)
Gary Thain (Uriah Heep)

Jean-Yves "Blacky" Thériault (Voivod)
Fred Thomas (James Brown)
Dougie Thomson (Supertramp)
Scott Thunes (Frank Zappa)
Jeremy Toback (Brad)
Michael Todd (Coheed and Cambria)
Peter Tork (The Monkees)
Fred Turner (Bachman-Turner Overdrive)
Kathy Valentine (The Go-Go's)
Ross Valory (Journey)
Joey Vera (Armored Saint, Fates Warning)
DD Verni (Overkill)
Tony Visconti (David Bowie)
Sid Vicious (Sex Pistols)
Eerie Von (Danzig, Samhain)
Klaus Voormann (Plastic Ono Band, John Lennon, George Harrison, Ringo Starr, Manfred Mann)
Jeff Walker (Carcass)
Jimbo Wallace (Reverend Horton Heat)
Jared Warren (Big Business)
Rob Wasserman (Bob Weir & RatDog)
Norman Watt-Roy (Ian Dury and the Blockheads)
Pete Overend Watts (Mott the Hoople)
Pete Way (UFO, Waysted)
Alex Webster (Cannibal Corpse)
Andy West (Dixie Dregs)
Jeordie White (Marilyn Manson, A Perfect Circle, Goon Moon)
Mark White (Spin Doctors)
Tal Wilkenfeld (Jeff Beck)
Leon Wilkeson (Lynyrd Skynyrd)
Lamar Williams (Allman Brothers, Sea Level)
Liam Wilson (Dillinger Escape Plan)
Kip Winger (Winger, Alice Cooper)

Tom "T-Bone" Wolk (Hall & Oates)
Chris Wolstenholme (Muse)
Chris Wood (Medeski Martin & Wood)
Ron Wood (Jeff Beck Group)
Allen Woody (The Allman Brothers, Gov't Mule)
D'arcy Wretzky (Smashing Pumpkins)
Rob Wright (Nomeansno)
Chris Wyse (Ace Frehley, The Cult)
Sami Yaffa (Hanoi Rocks)
Hiro Yamamoto (Soundgarden, Truly)
Adam Yauch (Beastie Boys)
Doug Yule (The Velvet Underground)

And as a bonus, here are 4 lines to add additional bassists who you feel should have been listed…but are not (and feel free to also include your own name if you're a bassist, too!):

1. _____

2. _____

3. _____

4. _____

Photographs

Paul McCartney
[Photo by Jim Summaria]

Bill Wyman
[Photo by Jim Summaria]

John Entwistle
[Photo by Jim Summaria]

John Paul Jones
[Photo by Jim Summaria]

Greg Lake
[Photo by Jim Summaria]

John Wetton
[Photo by Jim Summaria]

Chris Squire
[Photo by Richard Galbraith]

Geezer Butler
[Photo by Jim Summaria]

Geddy Lee
[Photo by Richard Galbraith]

Gene Simmons
[Photo by Richard Galbraith]

Dee Dee Ramone
[Photo by Richard Galbraith]

Glen Matlock
[Photo by Steven J. Messina]

Tina Weymouth
[Photo by Richard Galbraith]

Sting
[Photo by Richard Galbraith]

Tom Petersson
[Photo by Richard Galbraith]

Michael Anthony
[Photo by Richard Galbraith]

Steve Harris
[Photo by Richard Galbraith]

Billy Sheehan
[Photo by Steven J. Messina]

Cliff Burton
[Photo by Richard Galbraith]

David Ellefson
[Photo by Greg Prato]

Dan Lilker
[Photo by Steven J. Messina]

Flea
[Photo by Steven J. Messina]

Cris Kirkwood
[Photo by Greg Prato]

Bill Gould
[Photo by Greg Prato]

Doug Pinnick
[Photo by Steven J. Messina]

Doug Wimbish...plus Corey Glover
[Photo by Kurt Christensen]

Jeff Ament...plus Eddie Vedder,
Mike McCready, and Stone Gossard
[Photo by Steven J. Messina]

Mike Watt...plus Eddie Vedder and Dave Grohl
[Photo by Steven J. Messina]

Ben Shepherd
[Photo by Kurt Christensen]

Les Claypool
[Photo by Kurt Christensen]

Interviews

Billy Sheehan

What first attracted you to the bass?

When I was a kid, there was a guy named Joe Hesse - he's still one of my dearest friends. He was older though - I had an older brother and sister, so he was more friends with them. I was just a little kid. But he lived around the corner, and he was a really cool guy - he had a Triumph motorcycle, a beautiful girlfriend, and he was a bass player. And I kind of wanted to be like Joe. I looked up to him. And I could hear the bass…I was a little kid, so I had to go to bed early. I'd be sleeping in my house four houses away, and in his basement, they were rehearsing. Y'know how now you can hear a car coming down the street from a mile away if it has a strong subwoofer on it? Sure enough, I could hear the bass. One day, I went over, and he let me pick up his bass and I plucked it a couple of times - I got a blister on my finger! Right away, I knew it was a relationship that would go far.

So, I took my initial cue from him, and then when the Beatles came out and the world became crazed with music and bands, I managed to get ahold of a bass, and went from there. But lo and behold, I just loved the aesthetic of the bass - it was big, strong, and powerful, and the strings were thick and giant. And the sound was deep and low, and shook the whole building. Guitars are nice, but they have little strings and the amps were small, and they were shrill and harsh and high frequency. So, I just gravitated towards the bass.

Besides the Beatles, who were some of your other bass influences early on?

Paul Samwell-Smith of the Yardbirds. An unsung hero. He is such a great, great player. And he was really doing a lot of back and forth with the various guitarists of the Yardbirds, the ones that are famous - Eric Clapton, Jeff Beck, and Jimmy Page. But Paul Samwell-Smith was there for most of them, playing along with them. He did an amazing job. He is why I have the Gibson style pickup in the neck position on my Attitude bass - because of that low and deep, EB-O sound was one of my favorite bass tones. And the Fenders don't sound like that, really, so by adding that pickup on the Fender, I got both tones out of one bass.

And Tim Bogert was a big influence for you, as well, right?

Probably my biggest in a lot of ways. Because he really made the bass part of the orchestration of the song - as many bass players did back in the day. It's actually only recently that we've gotten into this mindset where the guitar player says, "Hold an E while I solo," and you hold a note for several hours, while they do their thing. Two problems there - guitarists should be able to play over changes, and a lot can't, unfortunately. I think they should strive to do so. And having a moving bassline underneath what you're doing makes everything better - which is easily demonstrated by any piece by Bach on a keyboard, where the left hand is accentuating and moving and changing the essence of what's happening on the right hand. You can do the same thing on the right hand, but if your bass notes move, it sounds different.

I remember we used to always talk about "the secret note." Y'know, the guitar player would be soloing away, and I would move to another note in that scale, and suddenly, his soloing becomes something different - even though it's the same notes, it's a different root note. It was always fascinating for me to hear that. I remember the Cream *Wheels of Fire* record, that iconic live record, Jack Bruce is moving around underneath Eric Clapton - it works and it's fantastic. So the idea that you have to play one single note and hold it while the guitar player has his way with the world, I'm not particularly in agreement with. So, it becomes a situation with me that a lot of guitarists get upset when they hear me move around, but most of the guys I play with enjoy it, and it was good and fun. It added to the musical depth and dynamics, instead of just being a drone/single note. And I'd say, "Well, then get a set of Taurus pedals. Just hold the E note, solo over it, you can send me home, and you'll save an airline ticket, a hotel room, and room on your tour bus, if that's what you want." It's a kind of interesting dilemma.

How did you come up with two-handed tapping on the bass?

Billy Gibbons. 1974. Alice Cooper with ZZ Top opening up, New Year's Eve, in Buffalo, New York. We knew the promoter, and he got us right up front - I think we made it to the first row. And as I was standing in the shadow of Billy Gibbons' cowboy hat, I was looking up at him playing - because we did a zillion ZZ Top cover songs - he bent a note, reached over with his right hand, and touched the fretboard. We all looked at each other, because no one had ever seen that before. Man, we thought, "Holy cow...*this is unbelievable!*" I went home, tried it on the bass, and wouldn't you know, it works! It's hard to go on YouTube now or anywhere and not see a guitarist tapping. But if you go past a certain year and look at videos by time, there comes a point where *nobody* did that. I mean, there were a couple of guys - everyone has seen the Italian guy [Vittorio Camardese, in 1965] doing tapping, and Paganini had parts like that on the violin hundreds of years ago. There's nothing new under the sun. But bringing it to light like that, I got pretty extensively into the tapping.

And then, [Van Halen's] "Eruption" came out, and I thought I was the only one that was doing it. Sure enough, someone else had mastered it, and Eddie deserves all the credit for popularizing it, and really making it what it is today. My influence pales in comparison to him. But nevertheless, it was nice to have come up with that and started utilizing that in various things. And I was playing in a three-piece band, and you needed as much as possible to make up for the lack of keyboards or rhythm guitar. The tapping thing turned into a way I could get a double piece of melody or whatever in there in the background, if I needed it to make a copy song sound more like the way it was supposed to sound. So, it was really an essential, handy, and useful thing - as opposed to just a gimmicky trick. But even to this day, I'm trying to come up with new things and new ways of playing, new techniques. That's a big part of my vocabulary. But a couple of times, I've done shows where I absolutely *refused* to touch the neck - on purpose. Just because I don't want it to become automatic.

How did you obtain the bass which later became known as "The Wife"?

That was my first bass…actually, there was a bass before that - a Hagstrom bass. But it was a toy. It was a tiny, three-quarter thing. When my buddy Joe saw it, he said, "I can put that on my key chain!" So I went down to Art Kubera Music on 910 Fillmore Avenue in Buffalo, and got my first bass. It was just awesome. The smell of opening up the case - I remember it to this day. I still have the original book that came with it - that tells you how to check the intonation. A little manual that came with it, and was signed it by the guy who assembled the bass, I think. Then, I saw Tim Bogert with Beck, Bogert & Appice, and he had what appeared to be a Tele bass neck on a P-Bass - on the cover [of BBA's self-titled album from 1973]. I talked to him years later, and that wasn't exactly what it was, but in my mind, it was.

So, I bought a '68 Telecaster bass - which would be worth a fortune now, back then, it was 200 bucks - took the neck off, and put it on my P-Bass. And I loved it, because it was big and fat and giant and sustain-y and beautiful. And then that bass also had the humbucker pickup installed in the neck position - the Gibson tone. I didn't know how to wire a switch when I put that on, so I just had two outputs, and ran two cords through two channels, so I had two cords to two different amps - and that's how it is to this day. It's a very handy way of doing it. It wasn't original - I didn't know at the time when I did it that there was such a thing as the Rick-O-Sound bass, which has a similar wiring. And also, all the Alembic basses years after that, when they came out, they were all wired with separate outputs for each pickup.

You mentioned the music store that you purchased the bass.

Art Kubera Music. It was an iconic music store in Buffalo. *Every* musician in town owed Art money - some of us paid it back. But what a wonderful, generous man. He was there to support the music scene in Buffalo from the '60s on. He really was responsible for elevating a lot of people's careers and playing. He was just a wonderful man - he passed away a few years ago. His son is still there, but unfortunately, the music store is gone. But he's one of those unsung heroes - the guy that runs a little mom and pop music store, and he'll let you buy something on time. You come in and pay him your 20 bucks every week, and you end up with a great amp, and you're a better player for it. Sometimes, we forget the kind of influence people like that have on us, and how grateful we should be for that.

And then, how did you get involved with Yamaha instruments?

Years of abuse and sweat and pounding and from a freezing cold truck to a hot club, it took its toll on that bass. The body has a hairline crack through the whole thing. It was just beat. I had a second one as a back-up made - which I refer to as "The Wife's Sister." She hasn't been seen much, but it was kind of the same situation - with a Tele neck, also. But I knew I needed something a little more reliable and I had done those basses myself, so they were kind of hacked together - because I'm by no means a champion woodworker, or luthier by further stretch of the word.

So, Yamaha contacted me when they saw some of the national press I was getting - about '83/'84/'85 - and said they wanted to make a bass for me. And they did - they did a BB-3000. It was pink-ish…actually, it was rose blue, but it turned out more pink than blue, which I caught a lot of heat for! But that's OK - the bass was great. It was nice, but it wasn't quite right - the body was a little wider, and it laid on me a little differently. So they did another prototype of their RBX basses. It was nice, but it was small and didn't really have any meat to it. Finally, a guy named Rich Lasner - he's designed guitars for a lot of companies - he was with Yamaha for a while, and he put together the Attitude bass, which was basically, "Use my P-Bass as the template."

So, all the knobs were in the exact same place, the neck position pickup, P-Bass pickup, we measured the '68 Telecaster neck as the template for all the necks, so they're all based around the dimension of that. And we did a few extra things that were helpful - one extra fret at the top, to get the high E note, that you could bend up to a G, and really expands the range of the bass. The neck to body joint was always a problem on the P-Basses for me, because I'd bend the neck for vibrato, and it would always come loose, and would even move in the middle of a show. So we made a neck to body joint that was rock solid - you can't move that thing at all. And that became my main bass, that I use all the time. Pretty much any record since then and every live show has had some form of the Attitude bass.

Which amps and effects do you currently use?

Right now, I'm using Hartke LH1000 - it's a big thousand watts of beautiful, clean power with not much on it. It's got a middle bass treble, and that's it. A balance control if you add different speakers, but it doesn't do anything to the tone. And the speakers they have now - the high drive speakers - are very similar to the old JBL's that I used, because I grew up playing JBL's mostly. I had woven in some Ampegs through the years, too. But mostly, I played through Pro Audio stuff for almost all of my life, because it just suited my needs more. Back in the way early '70s, I had racks of Pro Audio gear, as opposed to any pedals or effects like that.

So now, I have the Helix as the front end to that amp, because the Line6 people were kind enough to take an iconic-al pre-amp of mine done by Dan Pearce of Pearce Preamp, which has a very special tonality to it, unlike anything else in the world. And I used it on everything from 1979 until recently. And they modeled the Pearce component by component, and the results are glorious. So, I used the Helix Pearce preamps that are in the Helix. And all these other peripheral things in there - compression, and some high pass and low pass. So, things that I need for various things, they're all built in, which makes life so much easier.

So, it's the bass end of the Helix into the Hartkes, and it's been so predictable and so controllable. Last night, we [Sons of Apollo] played New York City, and a couple of friends of mine that always come out to see me were right up front. I wanted to make sure from them, "What do you think?" And they loved it. So, I'm very pleased with the sound of the set-up as it is.

I once read a quote from you that stuck with me - you suggested that beginner bassists start out studying the bassists of bands like AC/DC and Judas Priest, rather than aiming high right off the bat.

It's a tough time for people to get started, because with no guidance, you'll end up playing scales - which I'm not sure exactly what is what you need to do, to start. For me and everybody from my generation - because I'm an old man - we were the guys that all there was, was bands and music. There were no video games or internet or nothing. It was bands and music, and that was what it was all about, all the time. And all we did was play - play live and perform. Back in the day, I did 21 nights in a row. I did three full shows in one day - morning, afternoon, and evening. And we just played constantly. And we played songs. And we learned songs. And we sang, played, performed, and entertained people. I'm not putting myself in that category by any means, but that's what the Beatles did, that's what Van Halen did, that's what AC/DC did. Every great, iconic band that came from that era, that's what all of them did - they learned how to play *songs*.

So, I encourage people to learn some songs. If you're going to learn songs, I wouldn't start with something complicated - I'd start with something simple, like we did. We were playing "Gloria," "Louie Louie" - pretty easy stuff, but it's a great way to begin. And you understand what it's like to play on stage and play an actual song in front of people. It's worth its weight in diamond dust or platinum shavings. I just see a lot of players now that are like, "Hey, let's jam!" "What songs do you know?" "None." So, what are you going to play? You can't play a song from beginning to end? Guys that have been playing for five years - "Do you know *any* songs?" "No." "Can you play a song from the beginning to the end?" "No, I can't do it." It's sad to see.

Now, it's not everybody, of course. But I do believe that playing songs - sit down with a great record, and learn the whole thing. *Back in Black* is awesome. Judas Priest is great. I'm just using those, which are metal-y and heavy - not everybody is into that. Fine. So sit down and learn an Everly Brothers record. You couldn't get much better than that. Or the Beach Boys. Or the Beatles' early records. Just learn 20 Beatles songs - you'll be a better player, no matter what. And no matter what instrument it is. And sing it while you play it. Your career will do much, much better. *American Idol* and *The Voice,* they don't have bass players, guitar players, and drummers competing on that - they just have people singing. And singing is important - Paul McCartney, Lemmy, Doug Pinnick, Geddy Lee. Guys who sing and play. You'll always do better.

But I'm always trying to encourage young players to travel that path, because I do think it's a righteous way to go, and so many who have become incredibly successful have done exactly that. So, why not do what others have done, who are where you want to be? It makes perfect sense to me. However, of course, I'm an old guy, and I don't have all of the answers at all. So, maybe starting out and just playing scales for ten years, maybe that is a legitimate way to become a musician. It's not for me to say - it's art, and you can do anything you want, and any way that you feel is the right way is OK. But there is some craftsmanship that is required to write a song, to perform an evening. And I do believe that the best way to get it is by imitating the masters that came before us.

What is the trickiest or most demanding bassline for you to play?

Let's see…well, in Niacin, which was a band I had with Dennis Chambers on drums - who is the greatest musician I know on *any* instrument - we had a keyboard player [John Novello], and he would write a lot of lines that were great for keyboard, but on the fretboard, it was another story. And I don't think he was really used to writing lines with the instrument he was writing it for in mind. And that's true - a lot of times a classical composer, they understand the limitations or the possibilities of the instruments they are writing for, and they kind of fine tune their parts for that instrument. So, you can't play a chord on an oboe. It was really tough sometimes to play those keyboard lines in Niacin. That was a real challenge.

With Steve Vai, we did a song called "Freak Show Excess" off of *Real Illusions: Reflections,* which I played on. I got home, and I had to learn only by ear - I don't read music at all. So, I sat down and figured everything out, and showed him. "This is right, right?" "Yeah, this is right…but the fingering is wrong." He wanted me to finger it exactly the way *he* fingered it. So, I had to un-learn it - which is harder than learning it - and re-learn it with his fingering. That was tough. But it came out good - we played it live and it was cool.

And there are a couple of songs with Sons of Apollo too, that are pretty challenging. There's one song ["Opus Maximus"] that has a section of eleven, nine…I forget how it's actually configured, but I think it's three things of eleven and one of nine, and then eleven/nine/eleven/nine, and then back to three things of eleven and one of nine. It's not hard to play, but just to remember it and execute it every night in front of a live crowd is challenging. Again, that refers back to what I said regarding how good it is for players to be playing and performing in front of people, because sitting, recording, and punching in and out, you can do just about anything. But if you can do it live, standing on stage, while the monitors are feeding back, and there's commotion in the front row, then *that's* the true test.

Little known fact - you were jamming with Eddie and Alex Van Halen circa the early 21st century. Was it in hopes of forming a new band?

Eddie was kind enough to invite me to his house to play. I don't know what he had in mind, really. Possibly doing something - he alluded to that. There was no offer or concrete thing. But it was a great honor to go up and jam with Ed and Al. I'm not sure exactly when it was - maybe early 2000's. But I love Van Halen, I love Ed, I love Al, I love Michael, I love Dave, and I love Wolfie too, and Sammy's a good guy, also. I don't know what was going to come out of it, but that I ever got the opportunity to play with Ed or know any of them is a great thing. So, it was just an honor for me to go up there and play.

Ed called me later, and enjoyed what we did. Nothing came of it, but I got to do it, so I'm happy about that. And as a result, I'm the only guy in the world that has played with every member of Van Halen. Sammy, Dave, Gary Cherone, Ed, Al, Michael, and I even played with Wolfie one time, but he was a little kid, and I didn't play music - I was on a flight coming back with Ed from a benefit show, and Ed wanted to get some sleep, so I took over the babysitting duties, and me and Wolfie played with some paper and pencil, and did some word games and drew pictures. Hopefully, someday I'll get to jam with him!

Mike Watt

Let's discuss your bass influences, and how you discovered the instrument.

Tony Kinman from the Dils just died from liver cancer. The Dils was a huge influence on the Minutemen - they were from the old Hollywood scene in the '70s. He was just a huge hero to me. The idea of the bass could be on an even playing field with the other people of the band was really hammered home to us with the [punk] movement, because in arena rock, it was totally a hierarchy. That was where you put your retarded friend...it was like right field in little league, or something. Like the thing about John Lennon - Paul McCartney really wasn't the first bassist. There was a friend - I think a painter guy [Stuart Sutcliffe] - that John Lennon wanted in the band. I think that's kind of what it was - or it was guitar players who could play guitar good, but not as good as the other people who could copy better. So, they would take bass just so they could get a gig. It wasn't the first instrument - I think maybe in jazz and classical things, and R&B. But with rock n' roll, man, it was a hard time coming. And with the movement, for one thing, a lot of the cats were just starting out. So, they're all lame - the drummer, the guitarist.

    A lot of time, you listen to those old punk songs, the bass is driving it - guys like Dee Dee Ramone are writing the songs, Richard Hell is the leader of the band. This is completely different. The closest thing I could think of in rock n' roll, I've got to say, the English guys, Jack Bruce...well he's Scottish - this guy was really influential on me, too. When the movement came in, people like Tony Kinman - Tony 19 - were just amazing. Also, a lot of those Hollywood bands had women in the band, and a lot of them had women bass players. In fact, the first time I saw a woman in rock n' roll - not playing tambourine or being a back-up singer - was Suzi Quatro, opening up for Alice Cooper. She was playing bass and singing. It's interesting about the bass, and how I was very lucky to get into it. And having to say goodbye to Tony...you never get used to this shit, y'know? My pop, it was almost the same scene - the cancer taking this huge, strong guy. Man, it's not kind.

But Jack Bruce, he lived a hard life and made it to 71. I was on tour with the Italian guys - Il Sogno Del Marinaio - man, that was the hardest gig of my life. I found out right before we played, and then a member of the opening band let us konk at his pad, and y'know this game where you go on YouTube and you look at the videos? I listened to "Tales of Brave Ulysses," and man, I cried like a baby. I really owe these guys. It helped me realize that the bass...well, D. Boon was into it. Actually, the lyrics he thought were just thinking out loud, but he thought the real politics in the Minutemen - and Nels Cline talks about in the *We Jam Econo* documentary - that it was how the band was put together. Of course, coming from our experience with arena rock - we'd never been to a club until the movement. So, if anyone was going to make a change, it was going to be the guy who was kind of dominant - the guy who played guitar.

So, he got these ideas from the R&B guys, and he played very treble-y and left room for the bass, and don't use power chords, played jazz-y, ninths, elevenths, thirteenths, and diminished things, that would kind of not ring out so hard, and give room for the bass and the drums. And of course, I was into that. And we grew up playing together, so if it was one of his tunes - which meant he wrote the words and they rhymed - I could get those. But if they weren't going to rhyme, fuck no - I wasn't going to get that. And he never wrote a tune to my words. Both him and Georgie [Hurley] would really supply me and help me. I wrote some Minutemen songs on guitar, but I can't play guitar very well - the strings were too little, and I didn't really learn that much. But the bass coming first is an interesting thing, and it comes from D. Boon just being comfortable with that. I remember seeing something with Chico Hamilton when I was younger - he made records, and he would have songwriting credits. And people would be like, "Drummers can't write songs." *Why?*

And my favorite basslines, they weren't songs that went verse, chorus, bridge. No, they were *basslines*. And I think probably a lot of good R&B songs started with a bassline. But a lot of time, you need parts. And why can't a composition be like that - especially something like the bass, which is kind of part drums. I mean, it looks like a guitar, but the notes are where the drums are. I see these new kinds of things with six, eight, and twelve strings and shit...yeah, they may be up there with guitar, but mostly, bass stuff is where the drums are. But you've still got some notes, so you've got some form of melody without really being so adamant about the harmonies - like a piano or guitar - when you're showing somebody. Somebody like Nels Cline may love it - they see it as a launch pad or springboard. Other guys, it's not enough information - it's like you wrote the song on the kick drum or you wrote the song on the cymbals. It's funny about that. A lot of the way I play bass, it was first with D. Boon, and then the movement.

You know about the flannels, right? When I met D. Boon, we were twelve, and the only rock band he had ever heard really was Creedence. His dad was big into Buck Owens. And *Mardi Gras* [Creedence's final studio album, from 1972], fuck that one, but the six *real* ones - that's all we listened to, and we went, "I'm going to learn all this." Because right away, his mom wants to make me be in a band with him. Because it's in the proj [the projects] - we're from the needy houses in San Pedro. And it's the early '70s, so there's not a lot of guns, but there's fighting and stuff, so she wants us in the house after school. So, "OK, you're going to play the bass." And I don't really know what a bass is. I see on record covers that it looks like a guitar, just less strings. The first couple of years, I'm just playing the guitar with four strings. And I'm trying to hear the bass on the Creedence records. I'm looking at the covers and John Fogerty, and I'm from the houses, and I don't know lumberjacks and farmers and shit, so I just think that's his kind of rock n' roll shit. So, I thought, "If I wear flannels, maybe D. Boon will still like me, because I can't figure out this bass!" [Laughs] Now it's funny, when the movement comes…who is wearing these shirts at the punk gigs?

In Pedro, we had thermals - long underwear. '70s people were very orthodox. Probably more wild stuff maybe in Hermosa Beach - bell bottoms and stuff. But Pedro guys always wore this one kind of thing - all Levi's, and if it was fancy clothes, it would be Levi cords. So, to see this weird thing coming together of Creedence and Pedro, and this weird movement, where everybody gets to be in a band and make a gig, there was some kind of continuity. And that was a big trip to me about Richard Hell, too - in fact, I put a picture of him on my bass - I couldn't believe this, that a bass guy could actually run the band. *Really.* I didn't write any songs before the movement - except for one. It was called "Mr. Bass, King of Outer Space." I can't remember it all exactly, but it was about doing a bass solo that blew the rest of the guys off the stage. Obviously, I had some insecure issues about the bass, but now that I look back, I owe D. Boon's mom everything. It was the greatest thing in the world. But still, I get asked, "Why did you stop at bass? Why didn't you move on?" There's so much possibility still with four string bass guitar, I never moved. I do sometimes compose on the guitar - for Missingmen - because I want the bass to come second, that's all.

I know I'm kind of speaking free association, but that was a heavy thing on me - it was trippy that that happened right before I talked to you about bass, because I owe Tony so much. D. Boon - both guys. In fact, Tony said - because he was 62 - "I'm lucky. Look at D. Boon, he only made it to 27." 2018 is the first year I'm not touring in 35 years - just because I wanted to compose and record, which I'm doing. You get in autopilot mode and you stop thinking about things. So, when you're faced with mortality like that, when you're looking at a hero of yours being taken from you, and you think about all you owe him and you want to grow up to be him, and then I get to talk about why you wanted to talk to me - because D. Boon's mom put me on bass.

Let's talk about the basses and amps you've used over the years.

Let's go from the beginning. It was a guitar with four strings at some pawn shop - Tesco or Harmony. They were 10 or 15 dollars. I was 15 when I saw my first real bass up close. I remember it was the first year of high school, and I was bragging to some guy in home room, like, "I'm a bass player. I've got a band with my friend." D. Boon wasn't in my home room because of some alphabetical shit, so anyway, I'm telling this cat, and he sees me at the music store/record store, Chuck's Sound & Music. In those days, music was marketed much different - you'd buy 45 records in drug stores! I remember looking at this thing with four big old bridge cables. And I go, "Look at this thing!" And the cat goes, "I thought you told me you were a bass player?" And I said, "Yeah, I am!" And he goes, "That's a bass." And I go, "I know that!" I fuckin' did *not* know that. [Laughs] I lied - I felt so embarrassed. I thought to myself, "No wonder there are four strings - they're so fuckin' big." See, I didn't have the idea in my mind that the bass meant "low." Yeah, music now is way more accessible for people. We didn't have older brothers - no one let us on to this shit. It was like, "Oh...*OK.*"

And then, all of a sudden - James Jamerson, Larry Graham. You could really hear it in the R&B and the Motown stuff. And then, these English records, more and more - Geezer Butler, Jack Bruce, John Entwistle, and even dudes like Pete Quaife from the Kinks and Chas Chandler from the Animals. The English producers pushed the bass up. Even Tony Visconti - I know he's a U.S. guy - but he's playing the bass on [David Bowie's] "The Width of a Circle." I mean, it's *loud.* Trevor Bolder, Andy Fraser. So, when I start out, I get my first bass - it's a hundred dollar Kay. It kind of looks like the EB's that I ended up playing in the early 2000's. This motherfucker, you could put your arm between the strings and the frets. I mean, it hurt me to learn this motherfucker. I didn't like the finish - it was some red and black kind of thing, so I got a drill bit and taped on sand paper, so the thing had big grooves and valleys and shit. It looked horrible. So that's when I played with D. Boon in this thing called the Bright Orange Band. We never played our own songs - we just tried to copy Blue Öyster Cult, Creedence, Alice Cooper, and the Who.

I do get a Gibson, because we see punk - a band called the Bags, in 1977. He won't make a band with me at first, but then when I went and answered a Recycler ad and played "I Wanna Be Your Dog" for three hours - not even the chorus, just the one part - and I told him about it, he said, "OK, I'll make a band." So, we made a thing called the Reactionaries. And that's when I get a Gibson, and it's an EB-3L. I spray painted "PEDRO" on the front, and going to the gigs in Hollywood, people would see PEDRO and thought my name was Pedro! But one of the last Reactionaries gigs we do, I pass out from the heat, and I knock off my headstock. So, I've got to get another bass, and that's when I get a Fender. Because D. Boon had been playing a Stratocaster, and then he was playing a Telecaster, and I looked like you could walk on these things.

In those days, everything was in the Recycler - this paper that you could do free ads, and people bought it for 75 cents at 7-Eleven. You'd get your car, amps, basses, clothes, get in bands - everything - out of this. Anyway, Derf Scratch [of Fear] is selling real estate from his parents' pad at the beach in Santa Monica, and I bought my first Fender P from him. Only *Paranoid Time* is done with the EB-3. Then, all the Minutemen - up to and half of *Double Nickels* - is that Fender P. It's from the early '70s, with DiMarzio pickups. And I find a Fender Telecaster bass in Korea Town - you're talking Fender basses for three hundred dollars. It was set up like a PJ - the Telecaster bass was a '68 reissue of the first slap P-Basses in the early '50s. So, I get that and it had a big ass old bridge - Kahler made this thing for Fender called "The Claw." And this thing was like a boat anchor - it must have weighed two pounds, solid brass. I spray painted it - I used white epoxy paint for refrigerators. So that's from *Double Nickels* on the rest of

Minutemen, until D. Boon is killed in a van wreck [in 1985].

And then Edward [Crawford] comes from Ohio, and we do fIREHOSE, and I'm still using the Telecaster. But the body wasn't a Fender...actually, the only thing "Telecaster" was the neck and the tuners - because the body was actually one of these Schecter things that was swamp ash. This motherfucker was really heavy ash, and then it was cut for a PJ. Because those pickups, they had the little tiny ones, which are like a Fender Telecaster guitar. And then, me and D. Boon got into EMG pickups, because they were sealed in epoxy. We had a big problem as Minutemen - sweating a lot at gigs. And all the high end would shut out. But these pickups...they sounded terrible - they were very harsh - but at least it wouldn't lose the high end, because of the sweat, because of the epoxy. Otherwise, the wires came in from the bottom, so if you pounded on them, they would snap off. They should have had people like me and D. Boon to test shit - we really put the shit through the paces!

Anyway, I used that in fIREHOSE, until I find a '56 P-Bass in Hermosa. It's the last year of the little pickup. I guess the guy who sold it to the dude - we called him Hippie Bob, at Pier Music - and Hippie Bob sells it to me for 200 bucks, and it's got a big old hole where they guy tried to put in a bigger pickup. I was thinking in my mind, Tony in the Dils, he played a Thunderbird. So I didn't have a Thunderbird - yet. But I saw how big those pickups were, and I said, "I bet that would fill that hole," so he sells it to me for 200 bucks, and I put in a pickup. Chandler made their own version of a T-bird pickup, and it covered most of it. Some kid standing in line wrote "THUNDERBROOM" [on the back of the instrument]. But this is what I recorded on.

On one of the last fIREHOSE tours, the Beastie Boys asked us to play, on the *Check Your Head* tour - when they were playing their own instruments. Bitchin' album and a bitchin' tour...*not so happenin' audience.* [Laughs] The same thing happened when we toured with Primus - there are a lot of knucklehead/backward baseball hat wearing...not too enlightened. It was even worse than opening for Black Flag in the early '80s, if you can believe that - we're talking about the mid '90s, and you have these knuckleheads. The band guys were cool - that's why we were on the tours. But that's where I last used it. And then, in New York City, there was a case that was for an Aria Pro II or some bullshit, and the case said "Dee Dee Ramone." Inside there, was a Thunderbird II.

What happens is at a fIREHOSE gig, it was one of the last tours, I don't play it. Because what happened is I tried it for one gig, and then I pulled the headstock off! Gibson always had a problem - they get the tension on the strings by putting it on an angle. Leo [Fender] just cut out the thing - he didn't put it on an angle. And that always made them weak - especially the Thunderbird. And mine is a trippy one - it's a non-reverse. They only made these for two years. So I literally pull it off, and a bass has four hundred and something pounds of tension - I couldn't fucking believe it. So I do a bunch of repairs, and I had to splice on fiberglass and another piece of mahogany. That's another trippy thing - most Gibsons are made out of mahogany. And I get it going again. Even add a preamp - Bartolini - and it becomes the bass for the first opera [1997's *Contemplating the Engine Room*]. Which is really happenin' in a way, because that sound...it was a heavy record - I was dealing with D. Boon getting killed finally after how many years. So I detuned the E string down to D - D. Boon, D-string - and that becomes the bass for the first opera. And then I take it out on tour, and I do four tours of the opera with it. A little before that...I'm starting to hurt. In fact, this muscle, the one that holds up the bass neck [on the palm of your hand], it got about *this big,* man! Because the thing was so far out there, and lifting it up, and then the stretches. The Fender is 34 inches, and they're 34 and a half, so it's even a little longer.

In '96, I get this Larry Graham model - it's a Japanese version of a Jazz Bass, and Larry helped design it. And it's the most I paid for a bass, and I thought, "Maybe I should have something *that's good."* I tried one tour with it, and it wasn't really loud enough live, but man, for the intonation, the evenness of the notes, just such a great thing. I replaced the pickups - he had single coil jazz ones, and they were too buzzy, so I put each of these pickups that have four coil. I put in a preamp like I did with the Thunderbird, and I started changing and not digging that, so I made sure all my basses had bypass switches, so you can bypass the live preamp. There's something about pickups just going into the amp. And the same with the blend controls - I didn't want two volumes, because you never could get the mixture again. I was not digging the back pickups.

Yeah, there's more punch, and look at James Jamerson - he won't even take the cover off. So I only do one tour with it, and it just stays here. So these are my two recording basses - the '56 P and the Larry Graham. So now what happens too is these aren't really T-bird pickups. There's a cat named Curtis Novak in the desert, that I heard of through J. Mascis - he's a pickup winder. What he did was under this cover is a split cover - it's a P-Bass pickup. So he calls it a P-bird, instead of T-bird. It's got a coil here, and it's got a coil there - one for each pair of strings. So, with eight pole pieces - just like a Fender, like Leo did. I really dig it - he did such a good job. But that's really the only thing I changed from first putting in that Chandler.

The last Europe tour of that first opera in '98/'99, in Hamburg - it's North Europe, and it's wet - and man, after the gig, I can't hold the steering wheel. I've got to change, man. So, I go back, and my buddy here from Pedro, Dirk Vandenberg - who took the picture of *Double Nickels on the Dime* - has got a little guitar shop, and he sells me…remember my first bass, a Kay? And I did actually try a Mustang, but the Mustang neck was too skinny - it was like a Jazz scaled down, whereas the EB-0's and the EB-3's from Gibson, they're more a P-Bass scale, so the neck doesn't get skinnier. It had enough meat, but it didn't have the long-ness, and man, the pain went away.

Now, when you record you sit down, so it don't matter - you're right over the neck. So I always record with big ones. Strings are a problem with the little guys - the strings get flabby, right? So you've got to use heavier gauge - with the Wattplower…we'll get to that. But if you want to be in the game, you change. I mean, even techniques - when I did that fIREHOSE reunion six years ago, trying to do those old songs…you change. *It hurt!* As your hands change and stuff, your technique should change, I think - unless you want to do something that hurts you and makes you stop. So, I went to these little basses - EB-3, a '63. It got stolen. In fact, so did the Telecaster bass. So, I'm on tour with Nels and Bob Lee - it was the last US tour of the first opera. I never got that Telecaster again, but some boys here in Pedro had a band, and a guy gave me a bass, and that's what I used for the first years of the Stooges - up until 2008, because then all of the Stooges shit gets stolen in Montreal.

Right away, Adam Yauch gives me a Les Paul…oh yeah, I have to talk about my Gibsons, because in the old days, before the internet, even before *Vintage Guitar Magazine* - the stores don't know what each other have, so you're on tour, you can get a Les Paul Signature for two hundred or three hundred dollars. I got a '59 EB-2 with the banjo tuners in Bathesda in Maryland. And a Les Paul Professional that Adam Yauch gave me - they're not the best basses, but they are trippy and unique, and interesting. So, I have three or four of these Gibsons, that I don't really play. I have been trying to modify them - I put new pickups in those Gibsons. The Signature and the EB-2 are hollow, and there is something about a hollow bass. In fact, for Tav Falco a couple of years ago, I got a China Hofner - a "Beatle bass." And what a funny little thing that is - it weighs like three pounds, and flats.

But let's go back to I was using EB-3's for gigs for the Stooges, shit gets stolen, Adam Yauch gives me a bass - they are twelve pounds, those Professionals - and I play it once for a New York gig. Gibson wants to make me one...they started calling them "SG," and they're not that good, man. But I play this gig in San Diego...actually a guy from Rochester in Upstate New York, gave me a '69. And it isn't as good as the early '60s ones, but it was OK to do a bunch of gigs. But then, this guy named Dan in San Diego gave me a '65 - '63 and '65 are almost the same. And I put my own pickups in there. The problem I had with the EB's is the pickups - they're too muddy and they're in the wrong place. I like them in the middle, where a Fender P has got a pickup - and not 27k DC resistance, maybe 10 or 11, like a P-Bass. There is just something about it. I think bass was also kind of secondary for Gibson. But there were things that I liked about it - I liked the mahogany. It gave it a round tone and the littleness helped my soreness.

Now, Ronnie [Asheton] in the reunited Stooges played these guitars - there is a company in Toledo, called

Reverend Guitars. And he starts playing their stuff - they make him a signature model. So, they start coming to Watt gigs, when I'm coming through, playing. And they're like, "Hey Watt, we could make you a bass like this…that's better." I'm like, *"Yeah, right."* They take measurements, and the next year, I come through town, and they've got this prototype. I do it for the gig…it's terrible. [Laughs] It's got a lot of problems. "What's wrong, Watt?" "OK, this and that." So, they make changes, I come back around, and another one - we're talking five or six or seven prototypes. I thought they were going to say, "Fuck this guy!" But if your name is going to be on it, wouldn't it be something you would play? But they really wanted to work with me - Ken Haas and his design man, Joe Naylor. So sure, I'll try it. If you're willing to work with me, sure.

They bring back another one, and by about the seventh one, it was like, "Whoa, I can play one of these motherfuckers!" And by maybe nine, it goes to production - this thing called the Wattplower. So, the last couple of years, I've been playing these things called Wattplower by Reverend Guitars. It's a mixture. One problem I used to have by trying to put together a Fender sound with the Gibsons is the strings are closer together. So, you can't use a Fender P pickup with the pole pieces. So, what Joe Naylor did was make rail. And also, if you know about the Fender pickups, the pole pieces are always the magnets, so what he did was put the magnets underneath, like a Gibson does. It's kind of a hybrid - you've got the split pickup, but then you've got the magnets, and the pole pieces are bars, so it doesn't matter on the space. Also, it doesn't matter when I choke up on the strings - which you shouldn't do on bass guitar, but sometimes I do. That's what's good about playing in a trio, or Dos - you can do shit like that.

But they did other shit too - going through the body, having a brass spacer, because the way the Gibson, the angle of the neck, you can't have a Fender neck. But then that helps, because that big piece of brass, that neck dive shit is a problem. And that thing helped counter-balance. I like the Fender headstock, because I'm always getting out of tune hitting that D-tuner on the cymbals, because I like my drummer playing up front. A lot of shit comes totally from practicality - like the little body shape, because it just sits on you better. For me, I always called it "the lollipop" - there was something good about that little shape, so we worked with that. But basically, it's taking the best ideas I had with my Gibson and Fender basses. And them not having 'tude, and not saying, "You don't know what you're talking about," but working with me. Really not just trying to use my name or some weird shit like that. I really felt not lame about it. If you go to the Hootpage - mikewatt.com - there is a page with pictures of my basses.

Now, let's talk about amps. In the old, old days, when we're playing in the bedroom, it's a Vox AC-50. The guy next door to D. Boon, sells what I guess belonged to this LA psych band called Collidescope - it one 18 and 50 watts. I played that thing, and it was muddy as hell. When Minutemen comes and we're going to try and play in front of people - the Reactionaries, actually, and then Minutemen - I get something called a Peavey 400 - it's a 300-watt transistor, 2x15. And it's terrible. But I'm using a pick. And that's another thing - when punk came, it was a little too fast for me. Because I always did fingers, because Jack Bruce was using fingers. Well, I find out later that John Entwistle was using his fingers, pick, and slapping *in the same song* - it didn't matter.

I also found out that there are some "macho/sports things" about bass players that I can't stand. Because everything is vocabulary - when you're trying to put some dude down because he ain't doing what you're doing, fuck you, ass. At the end of the day, our job…I love the politics of bass - we look good making the other guys look good. It's aid and abet - whatever is gluing the shit together. We're kind of like mother-like. Most dudes, they go to the head [the bathroom], and as they're pissing, they looking at the tile. Well, we're the grout. We're setting that tile up. But man, you get these bass players by themselves, some of them get weird.

Anyway, I had to use a pick early on. In a way, using that Peavey amp, it was kind of like rhythm guitar - it didn't have a lot of low-end. But maybe for where I was with D. Boon and Georgie, it was OK. But then, the next amp I get, Acoustic gets back in the game. Because they were big in the '70s, but by the '80s, they went down. So they come up, and the big fad - here's another thing that bass players are susceptible to, fads - is called a bi-amp. So, like a PA, they're going to put all the low-end in in a bottom box of 2 15's, and all the higher ones in a box of 2 12's. So, this is the amp that I use for *Double Nickels on the Dime.* But, Ethan James, the producer man at Radio Tokyo, he thinks it sounds so shitty - he just takes it direct. That album has no mic'd bass amp. The thing is done on an eight-track - an Otari half-inch eight-track. He mixed it in *one night* - half the tracks had to be the drums. So anyway, I use that thing, and there's something about bi-amp that is funky, man, where you're standing - because bass develops far from the amp. Except, after a couple of years, I'm thinking it's the wrong kind of bi-amp.

So then, I get a Gallien-Krueger - an 800RB. I think it's got a 100-watt amp and a 300-watt amp. And I just got half a PA stack, and if you look at the back of one of the fIREHOSE records, you see it's an 18 top load, and then the top is 2 12's with a horn. Man, that was kind of brutal. And then, with EMG pickups in the Telecaster bass, again, Ethan doing the first fIREHOSE album [1986's *Ragin', Full On*] and the second one [1987's *If'n*], he didn't like the sound of this. I didn't like the sound either - just because you can hear, don't mean it's good. So, I give up on this shit. Up in Cruz, I'm doing a gig with fIREHOSE, and in a music store, they've got this thing called Eden, and it's just a tin box. And this is where I buy my first Eden box - in the early '90s. And he's also got an amp too - maybe it was called the PT-40 or something. But this is when I get my first Eden stuff, and I really get into Eden. And I'm *still* using Eden. This guy by the name of David Nordschow - his company is called DNA now. But starting with that one 210, I went to the 410 boxes, and I was using that E100WT, and then the Navigator going through the 50WT, where you have a separate power amp and preamp.

But there is something about that…you have to play good, because people could hear all the notes. [Laughs] If you were going to suck, you were going to suck *out loud*. In a way, it really helped my playing. But man, the weight. And especially after I hurt my knee…well, I was born with bad knees and had surgeries in my early twenties. But one of them went really bad about eight years ago. I mean, it's better than slinging a colostomy sack, so I ain't complaining. But I had to go for light weight. Luckily, David with his DNA company and neodymium - that new kind of magnet - I like it, because they act like fast attack 15's. So he came up with these 2 10 boxes that could do 700 watts each. I used two of them for a long ass time. Just recently, he came out with a 1350 amp - seven pounds, 1350 watts.

Then I found this company in England, called Barefaced - 40 pounds, 2 12's, 1200 watts. And then I use an Eden 12, 30 pounds. And I use a Crown Amp to power the Barefaced thing. So, I'm dealing with a couple thousand watts. One 410 Eden was 110 pounds. All three of these things together are 100! So this is where Watt's gone, and this is where I am today. Again, on my Hootpage, if you go to the end of my equipment stuff, you'll see a picture of my current set-up, and all these basses.

A lot of them I don't play all the time - they were part of this touring thing. Luckily, I got out of that - just to buy stuff. Luckily, they were econo. I'd see dudes like Edward in fIREHOSE come home with like, *twelve guitars.* [Laughs] You get an addiction just acquiring shit. For a couple of years there, I got some of these old Gibsons. Now, I only get shit that I play.

Glenn Hughes

What led you to the bass?

A long story...but I'll make it brief. I was named after Glenn Miller - the famous trombone player, who was also a captain, whose plane went down in the second World War. And since I was named after Glenn Miller, what was the first instrument I played? Well, it would be the trombone! The trombone led me to playing piano, and when I heard the Beatles in 1963, my mom bought me a guitar, which led to a few years later joining a band with Mel Galley - so I could play with my boyhood hero. That would have been when I switched to bass guitar.

You've played with many great guitarists over the years. Did you ever have to adjust or alter your bass style at all?

If I'm doing a record with Tony Iommi or Joe Satriani or Joe Bonamassa, they're all fantastic guitar players, and I've been very lucky to play with all great guitar players. But I think what they want from me, they want me to play like Glenn. I've been influenced by James Jamerson, Andy Fraser - my dear friend from Free - Paul McCartney, and Jaco Pastorius...the list is endless. So, I bring my style into it. I don't think it really differs that much, really. Even playing with Tony, it was all very "Glenn-sounding" - very melodic bass playing. So, I was very fortunate to retain my style.

Is it ever difficult to sing and play bass at the same time?

Not really, simply because when I'm writing, I'm always thinking, "Can I play this live?" But there have been a couple of songs in the '90s, where I wasn't thinking clearly, and I went to play them, and they were difficult. But now, for the last 20 years I have been specific about how I transform songs to the stage.

Is it safe to say that you are one of the greatest singing bassists in rock history?

Well, I'm very grateful. I really don't look at what people say too much, because I live in the moment. In the last few years, I'm still alive - where most of my dear friends aren't alive or they're not well or they've got problems and have had difficulties in their lives or what have you. And I have somehow escaped that. I've been clean and sober for a long, long time, and have a great relationship with my fans and family. But the fans are what draws me to playing live. I love a really strong connection with my fanbase.

Who were some of your favorite singing bassists?

Paul McCartney, of course. My dear friend, Jack Bruce. Geddy Lee is a guy who has been doing it a long, long time. Sting, of course - always remarkable. Changed the face of music in the late '70s/early '80s. Felix Pappalardi. I can go on and on. I'm just a real fan of music and musicians. I really like to listen to a lot of music, and I'm always listening to something new - so, if you can tell everyone out there if there is a singer who plays bass that I should be listening to, please, let me know!

Do you compose songs on the bass?

I have. [Deep Purple's] "You Keep on Moving" was written on the bass. When I'm writing in my studio, I've got acoustics and electrics and basses all around me, and it's like, when I'm with Joe and he comes over to my studio, we write. I'm writing with him, I'm playing bass, sometimes I'm playing guitar - it's just a matter of how I'm feeling at that moment. I do hear a lot of basslines. [Glenn's solo tune] "Soul Mover" may have been written on the bass. So, it just depends. I would say one in every twenty songs are written on the bass.

Which songs from throughout your career are you most proud of from a bass perspective?

A very good one would be "Black Country" by Black Country Communion - that intro. I always want to talk about the new songs rather than the old songs. I mean, don't get me wrong, I love the old songs, but I want to press the button and step into the new era. I've written a lot of new music. Y'know, "You Keep on Moving"…a lot of these things are really, really simple. Simplicity for me is a key factor. The notes I do not play are as important as the notes that I play. Those ones I leave out leave a nice gap for a nice fill on the drums or whatever. *I'm a groove player.*

David Ellefson

What originally led you to the bass?

I was a kid who grew up on a farm in Minnesota. Me and my brother got picked up at 7:15am every day, and we had an hour bus ride along the countryside, to go to school at 8:30, in Jackson, Minnesota. And the school bus driver - I remember in particular was the long-haired pastor's son, who was really cool - would always listen to WLS-AM, out of Chicago. And that was probably as close to what we would call today "active rock." They played heavy rock bands like Bachman-Turner Overdrive, Kiss, Foreigner, Styx - that was pretty heavy stuff for back in those days. And there was also a lot of pop stuff, as well - ABBA, "Afternoon Delight," Chicago - that was on the radio. Even though Chicago back in those days was a pretty heavy band.

As a kid who grew up watching shows like *Sonny & Cher* and *Donny & Marie,* to hear men singing with such aggression - especially Bachman-Turner Overdrive. That was like *death metal* back in the day - to hear Fred Turner singing as gruff as he did on "Let It Ride," and Randy singing "Takin' Care of Business" and "You Ain't Seen Nothing Yet." I always loved just how melodic it was, and I loved the harmonies, especially bands like Styx...and also Sweet, who had huge hits - between "Ballroom Blitz," "Fox on the Run," "Love is Like Oxygen." And ELO. I loved the vocal harmonies. I was always a kid who was drawn to melody.

And somewhere along the line, in and through all this, the instrument that stuck out to me for some reason was the bass guitar. And I always liked the way it looked. It was long, it had the four fat strings on it. I always liked the guys who played it - in particular, the first guy who I saw was Fred Turner on the Bachman-Turner Overdrive album, *Not Fragile*. A buddy of mine had the vinyl gatefold, so as soon as you open it up, there's a big band photo right there, of them on stage, and there's Fred playing this black 4001 Rickenbacker. It just looked so cool. You go from "I want to be a firefighter, I want to be a policeman" to "Holy shit...*I want to be a rock star."* [Laughs]

What are your thoughts on the whole pick versus fingers debate?

I think as a professional player, you need to be able to do all of it. You need to be able to play with your fingers, you need to be able to play with a pick, you should probably learn how to slap and pop. Probably my first experience with the pick was the big triangle pick. And for some reason, I just like the tone of it - more than anything. The guys on the records I was listening to, I know now most of them were recorded with flatwound strings, and my very first bass I got was a Gibson EB-0, and I bought it because on the back of the Kiss records, it said, "Kiss uses Gibson guitars and Pearl drums because they want the best." So, I begged my mom to buy me a Gibson bass, which we actually found in a newspaper in a neighboring town about 30 miles away. We went over, paid 150 bucks for it, went and bought a little Fender bass amp that had a little twelve-inch speaker. Brought it home, and I was so disappointed, because it didn't sound at all like Kiss. I was like, "What the fuck? Why doesn't it sound like 'Firehouse,' 'Cold Gin,' or '100,000 Years'? *What the hell?!"*

But I was self-taught...I mean, I learned how to play the Wurlitzer organ that my mother had, and took lessons from the church organist, and I took up tenor saxophone in the elementary school band, and played that all the way through high school. I had some formal musical education, so I taught myself how to play bass. I bought the *Mel Bay Electric Bass Volume 1 and Volume 2* books, and I sat in my basement, and I read manuscript and taught myself how to play the bass. But I wanted to play rock n' roll. I had enough musical discipline and enough education to know I needed to learn the instrument to play music on the instrument. But very quickly, I wanted to be in a band out gigging and playing. To me, I was never going to be "a bedroom bass player." I wanted to be out on a stage, rocking the nation. That was the goal from eleven and a half years old. I wanted to do what my idols were doing.

And right after BTO, certainly Kiss - the *Destroyer* record. I went on a family vacation to Seattle, Washington, to see some of my cousins, and we went to a music store, and I bought the *Destroyer* cassette, and they bought *Alive!* That *Destroyer* cassette changed my life. I just studied it. I mean, the opening line of "Detroit Rock City," with that killer bassline, I was like, "I definitely chose the right instrument!" I loved Gene Simmons, I loved the big, ominous, dark presence. It seemed to me that bass players had this looming, larger than life presence. And I loved singers and I loved the guitar players, but there was something about the bass player, that was the commanding guy in the band. Later, I think Frank Zappa said something like, "The instrument you play sort of defines you." And I always have this theory that your instrument chooses you - you don't choose the instrument. And that's exactly what happened to me. I feel like the bass chose me.

Which Megadeth song are you most proud of from a bass perspective?

Obviously, I'm a bit partial to "Dawn Patrol," because I wrote that. We had just come off the Dio/Megadeth/ Savatage tour, and Jimmy Bain and I had become friends, and I loved how Jimmy played and I loved his tone, and he was just a cool guy. He had a killer Yamaha endorsement, so he had all these basses. I went over his house one day over in the Valley in LA, and he let me take home his 8-string bass that he had. And that's what I wrote "Dawn Patrol" on. That was probably one of my first realizations that...it was almost that instruments have songs in them, and you just pick them up, and one day, the song falls out. Probably similar to how that "Peace Sells" riff fell out when Dave picked up my BC Rich Eagle fretless bass in rehearsal, and there it was. And I've had that experience with a lot of instruments over the years, where songs just kind of fall out of different instruments.

Back to that Gibson, I took those flatwounds off and I put roundwounds on - I bought some Fender roundwounds. I think they were nickel roundwounds, and I remember, this is before I learned that you are supposed to bend the string before you cut it. And I didn't bend it, and I cut the A string, and all the windings unraveled on the string. Because I lived on a farm three hours from Minneapolis and I couldn't ask my mom for another set of $20 expensive bass strings, I had to suck it up and play that bass for like, six months - with that fucked up string! But I'll tell you what - every single string I've cut since then, I always bend it before I cut it. Most of the best things you learn are from making a mistake.

But Gene Simmons...there is this ominous thing about bass, and I didn't even really understand it. For as big of a Kiss fan that I was, I really hardly ever played any Kiss songs on bass. They were very hard to play - I found them complicated to play. And the tunings were always a little odd - I later learned they would tune down a half step, which is why it never made sense in my Kiss *Destroyer* piano/vocal/organ/guitar book that I bought. Because I could read manuscript, and I was like, "Why are these notes all wrong, and I can't play it on my bass? There is no E-flat on a bass!" But all of that was just part of the education of trying to play.

Probably the biggest turning point for me is when I got my first bass at eleven and a half, and by the age of twelve, I was jamming with my brother's buddies and putting bands together. I was doing gigs - even if it was just on my parents' porch. And by thirteen, I'm playing semi-professionally at various events - whether it be paying my band a couple of bucks to play. That to me was what I wanted to do. To me, it was about being a professional player.

Do you agree that the bassline to the song "Peace Sells" has become one of the most iconic basslines in metal?

I don't know. I don't listen to it all that much. I think the reason that it has is because of the MTV thing. [For years, the channel used a bit of the song's bassline for their *MTV News* segments] Which look, it's a great bass part. And there is a lot of really great bass breaks inside of Megadeth. And you know who pointed it out to me, was Chris Adler from Lamb of God. He was playing drums with us in 2015 and 2016. We did a Knotfest down in Mexico City, and he says to me one day, "Man, it must be so cool to play all of these iconic bass breaks throughout the Megadeth set." I said, "What are you talking about?" He goes, "Dude, from where I sit, back here on the drums, so much of the set is really anchored around these bass breaks."

And I started thinking about it, and the songs during the set - "Dawn Patrol," "Poison Was the Cure," the intro of "Trust," there's a break in the song "Fatal Illusion" off of *Dystopia,* and it can go one and on. And obviously, the "Peace Sells" intro, and even on the *Peace Sells* album, there is another great bass break in the song "Devil's Island," where everything stops and this riding bassline comes in - this kind of triplet/gallop feel. Even the beginning of "Bad Omen," and the beginning and the verse part of "My Last Words." It's funny - Chris brought it to my attention, and then I started thinking about it, and I was like, "Wow. I guess he's right - there really *are* these moments where the Megadeth compositions turn a big corner, and the bass leads the way."

Doug Wimbish

What first attracted you to the bass guitar?

The sound. The frequency. The warm feeling that resonated through my body coming off records back when I was a child in the early '60s, getting into music and feeling the vibrations. So, I liked the tones. And also, the character that the bassist plays. It was all part of the persona in a sense - seeing a bass, a person playing bass. So, I got drawn into this as a child - the illusion of what it would be like to be a bassist. But also, I started realizing when I was younger when I would go to gigs, before I would get into the venue, I would hear this low-end - and it would be the bass. The shape of that note travels. So, all of the above. Being a young child, you're influenced by a lot of things. That's part one.

Part two was even before I was playing bass, I liked the sound of stringed instruments - violins, cellos, harps, mandolins. I had a mandolin first, and eventually, four strings broke, and eventually I had eight strings, and then four strings broke, and I had a four-stringed instrument - not knowing what I was doing. That started the idea of, "Now I have a stringed instrument." What was around me in the '60s was a lot of guitar players. '65 to '68 is when "the awakening" came, and it was a plethora of guitarists at that time - wanting to be Jimi Hendrix, Keith Richards, Wes Montgomery, and so on and so forth. Just a wide range of guitarists that were around. And I was attracted to the guitarists as well that were in my locale, and the local bassists that were in my locale.

I played guitar first and then switched to bass, because guitar is something that I could have access to and play. But it was being around an overabundance of guitar players in my area, and I was taking lessons from guitar players - not necessarily bass players - and those guitar players all had basses in their house. So, they were teaching me the songs they were playing in their bands. Like, "You play along. Here is the root note, while I play guitar. As a matter of fact, I'm going to practice my lesson with you, that your mom is paying five bucks for, and it's really for me to practice my songs in my band!" And eventually, that led to me being able to take lessons and learn more from guitarists - funk guitar players, rock guitar players. So, I evolved to be a bassist from playing guitar at first, and then playing bass with other cats.

It was all of that, and the timing of here I am in 1970. Jimi Hendrix just passes, the world is in a very interesting place, and at this point, I'm a freshman in high school - September 1970. It's a hell of a time going on. A lot of things were going on - rich and robust. So, I attach myself to all of that as a young kid. I became more attracted to bass, because I was around such great guitarists that I was learning, and was like, "I'll get my skills from these guys." I learned from all the local guitar players around here, that wouldn't play with each other, and I'm like that bassist that would play with a jazz guitar player or a rock cat, or a rhythm cat playing funk.

It wasn't like mom and dad took me to Guitar Center, and, "I want that one," and then I'm going to go and sit and watch some videos. No, it wasn't like that back then. Back then, to play bass, you played acoustic upright bass. There were no Mel Bay electric bass books, and if there were, they were very minimal. That's the era that we lived in. There was no MTV, there was no YouTube. There was just what was on the networks, and who were your heroes - who were your hometown guys. I'm from Hartford, Connecticut. I grew up around a lot of music and we had the second largest West Indian population at one point in America. So you had a very heavy West Indian influence, and you had a lot of rockers, a lot of Eastern Europeans, college radio - an abundance of resources. So you had to figure out a way to assess and get to that, and still not be caught up in the "band scenario," where you play with one band, but don't play with these cats. You had to avoid "the musical police officers."

How did you come up with your unique style of tapping and also using a wah pedal?

That all started at the same time. From '65 to '68 was a real deep time. A lot of records started getting really deep. Stereo started kicking in, and you were starting to hear wah-wah pedals for the first time, and fuzz. Whether it was the Rolling Stones' "Satisfaction," or Larry Graham playing "Dance to the Music" with distortion on it. And again, back to a guitar player that was one of my teachers, named Greg Gillespie. You've never heard of him, but he was like a Wes Montgomery/Kenny Burrell fanatic. But he was also a collector, so he had a Vox guitar that had a built-in wah and tremolo. I thought it was fascinating. And when FM radio kicked in, I loved to hear stuff in stereo. Like, listening to "Stairway to Heaven," the break section, all of Jimi Hendrix's records that were coming out, that were these deep-mixed records. I was too young to know what was going on, but I knew, "That sounds *great.*" Just the sound, spacing, and effects. So, I got into it early.

Also at this time, the Vietnam War is going on. One of our next-door neighbors had an older brother in

Vietnam, right in the heyday - '67/'68. And he would send his brother back the Chinese mock-ups of like, "Here's a Jimi Hendrix poster, a cheap little guitar, an amplifier" - made by, who knows? He was my next-door neighbor, so I would go over there, and we didn't know what we were doing - we would just turn it up, until our parents told us to turn that damn noise down. And then, his brother sent him a wah-wah pedal home - it was a wah-wah and a distortion. We got it to work, and I was like, "Wow, this is making even *more* noise!"

And then my other neighbor's mother was an artist, and she was deep into drawing and painting. The whole house was like an art studio. She was from New York City and worked in Greenwich Village. And her son, he got another amplifier, but his mom was into Jimi Hendrix. The first Hendrix stuff I heard was through my next-door neighbor. Fast-forward, my mother's side of the family is from the Bahamas, and I would go there for summer vacations, so in '68/'69, one of my aunts had a music store that was on the main street in Nassau. Half of it was a music store, half of it was an appliance store. And she had Fender basses, Fender amps, and during the summer, they close the store for a few hours, because it's too hot. And she would let me hang out in the store, while my grandmother was at the Straw Market down the street, selling baskets. So, I would have the whole store to myself, for two hours. I made sure everything was impeccably clean and back in the same exact location when I finished banging around on the drums, or playing the Fender Rhodes or the guitars. And she had a few effects in there, so I would play around with a wah-wah pedal. It was an evolution, again.

Then, when I finally had the opportunity to get a guitar, I bought one from my first teacher. I was always checking out his set-up, because he had a wah-wah pedal and distortion, and he would let me play through it. As soon as I got my first guitar, which was a Fandel - I believe Elvis had one while in the service. If I kept some of these instruments that I had when I was a kid, I could retire. Then, over a four-year period, I went from starting to play a little bit to being around the gear. And my older brother and sister, they had friends in bands, so my mom and dad would let them rehearse in the basement. I would come home from school, and there would be all this band equipment. So, I was around a lot of gear and music - between the Bahamas and America, at the same time.

In '70, a teacher let me borrow a Fender Mustang bass, and then a year later, he said, "I've got a couple of effects. Take this, and plug this in." The next thing you know, I started getting into, "Let me plug the bass into the wah-wah, and see what it sounds like." And then I would hear similar things on Sly Stone records. I then put the distortion on the wah-wah, and it sounded crazy. And the Fender Mustang had rubber strings on it. Then, he got an Echoplex, and I was like, "Man...*God just came through the door!*" I was able to be around guys that would let me try gear out. So, the next thing you know, I'm plugging in a distortion into a wah-wah, and that's going through the original Vox Echoplex, when you could feed it back, and get it to regenerate. I was in heaven. I would spend all day just playing and grooving. Then he got a Mu-Tron, and that was a game-changer - which was around '74. My whole era of when I started to play, I was into sound, stringed instruments, and effects all at the same time.

I was never like, "I've been playing bass for a while, I'm a traditional cat. Now, I'm going to get a compressor." I was like, "Fuck the compressor...give me a damn wah-wah or envelope filter!" If you can find the right frequency and it can make you groove, why can't a bass player have that? But I had to be patient, because at the same time, I loved how to play the bass. I'm like, "Give me a cable, plug it in, and I'm playing bass." In fact, my first recordings are just straight - my '72 Jazz going into a 24-track studio, with just a compressor or limiter. So, I learned early, "Find your lane and know when to pull stuff out." But, as I got into bands and as things started to evolve, then it became cooler when the bass became more of a forefront instrument. Like, Larry Graham doing his thing and popping, and Bootsy came out, and all these other players came out with sounds. Bootsy was envelope filtered, but he came from playing with James Brown for all those years. So, you know your lane, you know the job that's at hand, but if you can groove and you've got something that's sounding good, too, I'm down with it.

All that shifted in the '70s, where jazz cats like Herbie Hancock put out "Chameleon," and started to go electronic. Or Miles Davis got turned on to a wah-wah pedal because of Jimi Hendrix. Everybody gets influenced by somebody - whether it's fashion or by sound or whatever. So, Miles hanging out with Jimi Hendrix and seeing Sly play, after a while, he changed his clothes, big sunglasses, wah-wah pedal, Echoplex on that trumpet. A lot of cats were like, "It's about *the sound.*" So, we have a lot of musical police officers out there, that like to keep things traditional. But let's look at the reality of how time is - electronic music has only been around not even a hundred years, really. Things have evolved. We are all tested by the water that we're around. And somebody has to punch a hole through this stuff, and when you do it and something musical happens, everybody is like, "Yeah, I'm digging that!" Bootsy Collins, Larry Graham, Stanley Clarke, Jaco Pastorius, all these guys are great players, but they changed the sonic game for bassists. And I was that kid that just happened to be coming up at that time.

I worked with Miles Davis, and he was like, "I'm not going to play any more of that old music. That's 'dead man's music' - I've already been there and done that. I'm trying to move ahead." It's the people that you're playing with and the music that you're doing requires the coloring that you need. I just did a session in New Orleans with Tab Benoit - he's like, "We don't need any pedals. Just plug into the board and let's go." And in that scenario, you learn the song, and then you play it back three times, then you're recording it. There's no time for error. The whole record was done in two days. Other folks are like, "We're going for something that's deep," and they start mapping out stuff pre-production for a while.

Effects can give you a certain character, as well as what is coming out of your hands and your brain and your body. How do I want to have my bass sound? Am I a Fender Jazz player with no passive pick-ups, roundwound strings, coming out of an active amp? Maybe I'm more traditional, and I want to keep it down, give me an Ampeg Fliptop or SVT, and I'm good. It all depends on where you're at and how much range you're trying to produce out of the bass.

I was fortunate enough to see Jaco Pastorius - right before the *Heavy Weather* record came out. I was actually in the studio with him - I lucked out, because he was playing in Hartford and he was playing with Herbie Hancock's band for a brief moment, and I met him backstage at the Bushnell, and I had a conversation. I was about to sit in my seat, and he's like, "No, you can watch the whole gig *from here.*" So I watched the whole gig a few feet away from him! And right before that, he was like, "I just came out of the studio with Weather Report in Miami." He had the entire *Heavy Weather* record on a Maxell tape. He's like, "Would you like to hear the record we just finished?" So, two other guys from the local radio station happened to be there as well, and their station was right next to the Bushnell, so I went to the Bushnell, saw the concert - his playing was phenomenal - and then after that, I heard the entire *Heavy Weather* record.

Jaco had his Ampeg amps and this looping thing, but he was like, "There is a place here I heard about, called ElectroComp, and they have a synthesizer bass that they're working on" - because John McLaughlin had told him about it. I'm like, "It just so happens I know the guy. I can take you there." The next day, I pulled up in my Pinto, drove him out to the place, and the guys freaked out - they didn't know I was bringing Jaco out. They had retro-fitted an acoustic Ovation bass - this is '77. This company also does government contracting for Polaris submarines and sonar. They use the company for, "We need you guys to come up with a way to put something in our submarine so that if there are whales in front of us, we can disperse them through sending out tones." But on the side, they also experimented with synthesizers. So, I brought Jaco out there, and lo and behold, they had one of the first bass synths, and he was experimenting with it. So I was around cats that were killer players, but they were about *the tone.* All of this went hand in hand.

So, back to the root question - I got into sound early, and I got into effects early. And it's been parallel with me - depending on the events that I go into. But over the years, cats know I like effects - Joe Satriani gave me my first whammy pedal, doing his session [for 1992's *The Extremist*]. That changed my life. He had given me one of the first prototypes, before it even came out. I ended up putting that on Annie Lennox's *Diva* record, on the song "Precious." Everybody has their favorite pedal - I worked with Lauryn Hill, and out of all the pedals that I have, her favorite pedal is a discontinued DigiTech Synth Wah, that will blow everything up if you don't know how to use it. So, you never know what resonates through somebody's body, and *"That's* what's turning me on." It's because bass has such a frequency between harmonic chimes that I was turned on to by Jaco Pastorius, and you have that going through a little bit of chorus…that's heaven.

But then again…*I'm* the effect. I don't need any of these pedals. Don't even plug me in - give me a piece of wood and a string, and I will start getting into the frequency of it!

Glen Matlock

Were you originally a guitarist, or did you start with bass?

I started out on the acoustic guitar, and I still do that - every song that I've been involved with writing, I've written it on an acoustic guitar.

So you've never written a song on the bass?

Riffs and things that have come up, you can't really work out chord changes on the bass. Sometimes what I like doing, if you're in a band, you get a bass riff, and then you get the guitarist playing the chords that go with the bass riff, and then once you've got that down, you change the bass to do something a little bit more adventurous, hopefully. It works like that. I've been writing songs for 40 years, and I still really don't know how you do it. You just do each one as they come along.

You were one of the few punk bassists at the time to play with your fingers, instead of a pick.

It's cheaper. [Laughs] No, I think you get a warmer sound out of it, somehow. You don't have to look for a plectrum. That's what those little pockets in Levi jeans are for I think - plectrum pocket. You call them picks, we call them plectrums.

Were you playing with your fingers because you were primarily influenced by bassists who played with their fingers?

I've never really analyzed that. I must have picked up on it for some reason like that. But now thinking about people who I liked as bass players, they actually all played with a plectrum. I liked Ronnie Lane, McCartney's a good bass player, Entwistle...I'm not quite sure if he used his fingers or a pick. Nick Lowe is a good bass player, I like the bloke in Can, Holger Czukay, I also like James Jamerson - no idea if he played with his fingers or a plectrum. I like Klaus Voormann - no idea [if he played with his fingers or a plectrum].

Which Pistols song contains your favorite bassline?

"Anarchy in the UK." In fact, I remember doing that the last time we toured, and Duff McKagan was there, because he was playing with his other band, Velvet Revolver. And he knows Steve Jones, and I know him a bit, and he came up, and said, "I didn't realize you did all that sort of 'Tamla stuff' on the bass when you're playing on 'Anarchy'!"

Which basses and amps did you use with the Pistols in the '70s?

I started off with a Fender that Steve Jones gave me, but it was a bit of a plank, to be honest. And then I got a Rickenbacker, and that was a bit too "fiddly" for its own good. I've still got that one - it is now in the Rock and Roll Hall of Fame equivalent in Liverpool, on display. But I've had a few different basses over the years, and I've always come back to the Precision. If you're touring and you can't be bothered to lug a guitar with you, you just say, "I'll get a Precision," and they're the same everywhere you go, pretty much. They're reliable, dependable, and look like a bass guitar. I think a bass guitar should look like a bass guitar. Otherwise, I've always been a Fender man. I've got…it's not the original one I had, but it's a Fender Bassman amp and cabinet, and it's great when it's working properly. It's a bit like in England, you could say it's like the Mark 2 Jaguar of bass amps, and maybe in America, you could say it's like the Studebaker of bass amps. But it's got a really nice, warm sound. Ampegs I've always found have got a little bit of a growl, that you can't dial out.

Who would you say were some of your favorite punk bassists?

Punk bassists? I don't know if I really had any. I thought Paul Gray - who ended up playing with the Damned - was very good. Just after punk, there was a girl named Sara Lee, who played with the Gang of Four - I thought she was good. I like Tina Weymouth…is she a punk? I don't know. There's something about when girls play bass - it's more melodic. But I wasn't influenced by punk bassists - I like to think that *I* influenced punk bassists. It's the other way around. And I'm much more interested in the people I mentioned earlier, like Entwistle and McCartney as bassists, and Carol Kaye, James Jamerson. It's all the twiddly bits that make it.

Do you feel that Steve Jones did a faithful job of replicating your basslines on *Never Mind the Bollocks*?

Not really, no. He made it too "black and white." I think the perfect Pistols album would have been - the quality of sound - was the bass playing that is on the outtakes album, which is called *Spunk*. I maybe used to overplay a little too much, but subsequently when we played live, I did it in-between a bit. I put some more fiddly bits in hopefully the right places.

How would you rate Sid Vicious as a bassist?

He was a good *singer*…that's my answer!

Doug Pinnick

What first attracted you to the bass?

I was about four/five/six years old, and I remember hearing "Why Do Fools Fall in Love?" by Frankie Lymon and the Teenagers. It was probably 1956. I was born in 1950, so I was six. I remember I was really small, and I was sitting on the couch at my cousin's house, and they put the record on the record player, and I remember the bassline, and thought that was coolest thing I ever heard. From that day on, that was the interest - the bass. I listened to bass almost all the time on every song, and vocals - everybody listens to vocals, and I was a singer, so I listened to vocals. But the bass and the vocals were the two main things I listened to. I didn't realize there were other instruments. Nowadays, I go back and pull out the really old stuff I used to listen to as a kid, and go, "Oh wow, I didn't hear that drum part there. I didn't know there was a sax there." Literally, I homed in on two things - *for years.*

I remember you once saying that Chris Squire from Yes was a bass influence.

All that came later. See, I've been a bass player all my life - I just never picked it up until I was 23. I had a broom in the house and things that I walked around "playing" like I was playing a bass. And it was always left-handed - I didn't know any better. I never actually saw a real bass until I was probably in high school. And after that, I saw bands play. But I was oblivious to it, even though I was obsessed with it. We didn't have pictures of it, we didn't have rock magazines or anything. But I just knew that's what I loved to hear. And something made me want to mimic it. Then, later on, when I was around 21 years old, that's when I started to really see the bass players.

I was 23 when I started playing bass, and that's when I really started looking at other bass players, and getting inspiration from them, to figure out what I wanted - playing through an amp, getting a bass, and understanding, "Oh, *this* is how you play it. Not only do I like to hear it, but I've got to put my finger *here."* It was very exciting. And bass players in soul music, there was always James Jamerson from Motown, and Donald "Duck" Dunn from Booker T & MG's and the house bass player for Stax, and Chuck Rainey was the house bass player for Atlantic Records. So, all the soul music that I heard was those three bass players. They all played very similar, and that was always the mindset in my head, because that's all I knew. So, that's what I heard and played - or tried to play.

Then, Chris Squire came along, and that was like, "Oh, wow. This is something *completely* different." And also, Roger Glover from Deep Purple, the *Machine Head* record, I learned that backwards and forwards. That was when I really sat down and learned a whole song, and it was fun - just sitting down, getting through a whole song, and really piecing it all together. All those basslines on *Machine Head,* I grew up playing - those are my favorite licks. I met him, too, and did an interview with him. It was pretty cool - he's a King's X fan, too, so it was awesome talking to him.

Your trademark in the '80s and '90s was a 12-string bass.

That was not a trademark - I just used it a couple of times, and it was in almost every video that King's X did. So, all of a sudden, I'm "the guy who plays the 12-string." But the truth is - and everybody who plays bass knows - that Tom Petersson had been playing 12-string since the '70s. *Exclusively.* I've never seen him with another type of bass but 12-string. And he's the guy that really put it on the map - as far as I'm concerned. But I'm the one that seems like everybody knows, because I guess I'm the frontman of King's X.

But literally, by the third record [1990's *Faith Hope Love*], I played it on about four songs. And the fourth record [1992's self-titled], I played it on five songs. After that, I kind of put it away. I never really used it a lot. But I do love it, and I'm one of the few bass players that utilized it. Jeff Ament did also, with "Jeremy." I used it more, but I wouldn't say that I brought it to the forefront…you can say that if you want to, but I didn't. [Laughs]

One of my favorite King's X basslines utilizes the 12-string though, which starts the song "Out of the Silent Planet," off *Gretchen Goes to Nebraska*.

Well, it was actually an 8-string on the record. I didn't have a 12-string at the time. This guy gave me an 8-string. He made it, and said, "Do you want this? I can't sell it - I don't know what to do with it." It was like, 1988, and I brought it into the studio, and used it on "Out of the Silent Planet" - when Ty wrote that song, the beginning part, I made that riff up. People think it's a 12-string, but it's not - it's an 8.

When I interviewed Billy Sheehan for this book, he mentioned you as one of his favorite "singing bassists."

He tells people that I'm one of his favorites. [Laughs]

That's awesome. I don't understand it - I think we admire each other, because we're such polar opposites. We did a clinic together one time, and it was really interesting, because his approach to bass was 100% opposite of mine. So, it was really cool to sit and talk about the differences between us, and talk to the kids about it, and answer their questions. We shared with everybody that there is a whole spectrum of playing bass - different techniques and ways to do it. I think it opened the kids' eyes up a lot. And at the end of the clinic, we jammed - I played a groove, and he played lead. We looked at each other, and said, *"This is what we do."*

Is it ever challenging to sing and play at the same time?

No, not anymore. It never really was. There was one song that I could *not* get - "One Thing Leads to Another" by the Fixx, when we were doing cover music. I could not play that bassline and sing at the same time. I tried and tried and tried, and could not get my brain to sync up. But other than that, I usually don't have a problem.

Which King's X songs are you most pleased with from a bass perspective?

"Black the Sky" was one of my favorite bass parts, because it was just fun to play. For the 12-string, I think "Pray" is a lot of fun to play.

Your current set-up consists of a signature bass, amp, and pedal.

Tech 21 made me a signature bass amp first [dUg Ultra Bass

1000], and then there was a bi-amp, the way I run my amp and the way I EQ it, and they nailed it. It's very versatile, too - I'm really excited about it. No matter who plays through it, you can dial into it exactly what you want - it's not just a one-trick pony. And after a year or two, they made the pedal [dUg Pinnick Signature Bass Distortion Pedal], which is a very small pedal, but sounds exactly like the amp. To our surprise, people are completely losing their minds over it. So many people are buying it and saying they are throwing their whole rigs away, and other people are saying they are just going to play through the PA from now on, and soundmen are going, "This is *so* easy." I'm hearing all the feedback that I wanted to hear.

The Schecter bass [dUg Pinnick Baron-H Bass], it's basically a semi-hollow body Baron bass. It's black and looks kind of like a Telecaster, and it has two pickups in it. They asked me if I wanted it as a signature, because I loved it so much, so I asked them to modify it to put one knob on, because I don't use two knob controls at all - I just use one, wide open. The bass is also very light. It's a pretty bright sounding bass - it sounds more like me, than a normal bass. It's not a thick, deep-sounding bass. It's more of a bright, treble bass, like my tone is. It matches really well with my amp. I used to use Seymour Duncan pickups that they stopped making - they're really high-powered. They wouldn't make them anymore, so I've had them for like, 20 years, and kept swapping them out. But one day, I just put some regular old Seymour Duncans in everything, because with my dUg amp, it gets everything I need.

Any advice for fellow bassists?

My advice has always been - whether anybody believes it or not - the bass player is the most important part of the unit.

Our job is to lay a foundation, so everybody can dance on top of it.

John Myung

What first attracted you to the bass?

I started playing as a result of a good friend of mine that lived a house away from me, and he was a bass player, and the only experience I had up until that time was taking classical violin lessons and piano. I went for it, and I discovered it was a really great thing, and is something that I stuck with, and started getting really into rock music. Bands like Rush, Yes, Sabbath, Jethro Tull - all the classic '70s prog bands. I really connected with it. It seemed to be the right path to me. It hit me in a real way where there was no confusion as to what I wanted to do - as soon as I started listening to bands and playing in a band.

I learned playing from records, and after high school, went to Berklee for a year, and that's where myself and John Petrucci hooked up with Mike Portnoy - who is also from Long Island, but he was from the other side of Long Island. We were on the north shore, he was in Long Beach, on the south shore. I think that's what it is - when something really hits you in a profound way, things become very clear. That was a sign of something really truthful for me. It was embracing something that was really real. I've been on that journey ever since, and it's still going.

How much practicing did you do initially?

After school, you get home around 2:30 or 3:00, and I would probably go straight until 6:00 or 7:00 - just playing to records. It was either that or jamming with friends. And then after dinner, I would sit around and play to records. It wasn't really regimented, but it was something that occupied my time, for sure.

Did you take bass lessons, or were you just applying what you learned from the violin and piano to the bass?

For the most part, just self-taught. I learned by listening to bands that really meant something to me. It wasn't like I learned a lot of things that anyone told me I had to learn. It was just, "Well...what do I like? I like Rush, Maiden, Yes." So being that I liked those bands, that's the music I focused on learning.

Do you still practice?

Yes, of course. You have to play, or I feel like I lose some things. It's just an ongoing thing, where I don't feel right if I don't play. There's something about putting the time in every day, and staying connected with music. That is really important to me, because it simplifies things for me. And I try to keep things simplified - try to stick to a groove, stick to a routine, try to find different ways of thinking, and being open to other influences. It takes up most of your time - between touring and recording, and learning the ins and outs of what you can do with personal studios now. It's all very time-consuming, but all very good. You just have to pace yourself through it.

What did studying at Berklee do for your bass playing?

It turned me on to other styles of music. The most interesting thing for me was the people that I met. There were people that were into jazz, punk, avant-garde, pop - all different styles of players. Really great players. It was cool to be able to be part of this big melting pot of musicians from different parts of the world and different styles, and connecting with them on a social level. There was definitely a common theme - *music is music.* And there were all these different ways of interpreting it and expressing emotion. I didn't really stay there long enough to focus on any one particular thing, but it was just a great place, great resource. I used to spend as much time as I could in the library - listening to old recordings. It was a place where I could do just that, and get into a groove where you woke up, took classes, and from 6:00 at night to midnight, we jammed every night.

Which songs from your career have your favorite basslines?

I don't know if I connect with my basslines that way. I think more in context with what I'm contributing to the song and what type of song it is. When I look back, our most successful album was *Images and Words,* so I would tend to think whatever we did as a band that connected with the most people would be the most meaningful things that I've done.

Do you approach your bass playing differently in Dream Theater to Jelly Jam and other projects?

I approach it the same way. But I think what is different about it is the biggest thing is every musical situation has a certain chemistry, and a certain vibe as to what will work. I approach everything the same way - I'm just being myself. I have a sense of ideas that I'd like to use at this time. But I would say the end result is different, due to the chemistry - each band has its own unique chemistry.

What was your bass set-up for the *Images and Words* album?

I used a red Spector 4-string. In the studio, I left it up to the producer, David Prater, to get the bass sounds. It was a real kind of simple thing - a lot of it was direct, just through a DI. And then he had me going through...I think it was a Bag End cabinet. He may have had it going through part of a Marshall combo head. I don't really recall exactly, what the set-up was for my tone. But I do have the bass. It was more or less just a direct signal - it was more of a line level thing. There wasn't a lot of processing going on.

What about the bass you use now?

I'm playing a Bongo bass. And exciting things are happening, because I'm actually working on a custom model with them at the moment. So, hopefully within the next year or so, it will be available. I'm back to playing Music Man basses. I did the first album with a Sting Ray, and for the past ten years now, I've been just playing the Bongo basses, and working with them on a custom level. There is something about the Music Man basses that have always made sense for me to play - it stylistically works, because I play with a strong attack. If you're a finger player, and playing that sort of "Steve Harris style" - where you have a rhythmic aspect to the attack, and how you get tone out of the instrument - it seems like the Music Man basses compliment that stylistic playing the best for me.

What advice could you give bassists who may be trying to figure out a complicated bass part?

Now, with computer technology, get yourself some recording software - whether it be Pro Tools, Cubase, or Logic - and get to learn it. They pretty much all do the same thing. The only difference is people have opinions over which sounds better. But they all do the same thing, and it's just a matter of figuring out the functionality of whatever piece of software you chose. And within those applications, the ability to slow things down - the best thing to do is slow it down, break it down, and write it out in a way that makes sense to you. Start slow until it's comfortable, with a goal in mind being able to play it at the true tempo of the song. That's a great way to learn. It's such an incredible tool now that wasn't available when I first started playing. And when you slow it down, it maintains the integrity of the pitch. Although the passages are getting slower, nothing is getting detuned - it's still staying in tune.

It can be pretty confusing when you practice, because it's like, what do you work on? There are so many different things to work on. Do you want to master scales? Chords? Rhythms? I've been in a situation where sometimes you can feel really overwhelmed by something, and I find myself sometimes getting sidetracked, where I'm learning a scale or spending time on technique. The bottom line is, do you have anything to contribute to the song? For me, my playing and practice and what I try to focus on, I try to make things simple so that I can visualize what it is that I want to do - as a result of the time that I'm putting in. That visualization is simply playing my instrument with the goal of being inspired by something, that will inspire me to play something, that I would want to record and save.

For this new album that we're working on now, I have the luxury of being able to chill at my personal workspace, practice, and record as ideas hit me. And over a six-month period, I had six hours' worth of inspiration, so I think I was averaging like an hour a month. So, 15 minutes a week was the average of inspiration where I was playing, and all of a sudden, I felt, "This is worthy of being recorded. I feel really good about this." That's important to have that sort of dynamic with the instrument, whatever it is you're working on - it could be a piece of classical music or a favorite track from one of your favorite bands. There will be a point where you will be inspired, where you do something cool, and the best thing to do when that happens is to record it.

Because when you step into a writing session - in my case, I'm working with four other people - that captured inspiration is very useful, in terms of, "Well, what do you got? Play me something." For me, I need to have stuff captured already, as you walk into a writing session. You can't expect that happening the minute you start it. There is a sense of preparation involved for me, before we start an album. And then there is the whole process of breaking down what you did and organizing it and learning it - that's just as time-consuming. You have to listen to yourself play and edit yourself, because eventually, you'll get to something where you're like, "Wow, that was great. I'm going to save that. I'm going to learn that."

Writing with a group of people is really cool, because things happen very quickly. It's like, "You do that, you do this. Let's try this. Let's cut that in half." It's all in real time and it's all very spontaneous. So, being a musician today, the whole process of recording, inspiration, and organizing it and learning it, and applying as much of it as you can...the reality of it to me is you can generate a lot of ideas. Close to 200 little things that you think are cool, but at the end of the day, there's maybe three or four things that are actually really useful, and things that actually get used. So, that's how I keep myself busy.

Cris Kirkwood

What first attracted you to the bass?

As all things rock n' roll, in a lot of ways - especially for people my age - a lot of it goes back to the Beatles. Those guys reach was so incredible - as a toddler, I was conscious of the Beatles. And Paul playing that Hofner - it was obviously not a six-string guitar. It was a different animal. But when I really got around to thinking about playing one, it came out of *Guitar Player Magazine*, probably. That was around back then.

And I had been playing banjo for a while - I started playing banjo when I was about thirteen. And there was something about the way basses looked, and I suddenly started feeling it was cool around 15. They just looked neat to me. And then I thought it would translate over a little bit - just the right hand on a bluegrass banjo, the fingerpicking you do with a bluegrass banjo - to my ability to play a bass, fairly easily. Just because I kind of had my thumb and my two fingers involved from the banjo. And then there was something definitely intriguing about it being even a string less than a banjo - a bluegrass banjo has got five strings. I got taken by the look of the bass. I suddenly thought there was something intriguing about it.

I recall you once telling me that your two main bass influences were Phil Lesh and Dusty Hill.

I came up with "the psychedelic bass coin" - two sides of it. Ultimately, there's a lysergic influence that permeates my reality - and definitely my musical reality. I so clearly recall having played for a while, and then one evening, getting to a very "heightened state" through chemical enhancement, and really bonding with the instrument - that was like, *"Wow...very far out."* And not very hard to play, in a lot of ways - it's all one note, you don't have to learn chords. It's not hard to physically play the thing. And boy, there was one night at mom's house when she was out of town, and we were all just tripping balls, and Jesus, I just about got as far as I've ever gotten on the thing that evening.

You have Phil who is coming from a background of theory and composition. Actually schooled. So he's bringing that to the instrument. And doing "support bass playing," without writing on the one so much. He's not just hitting that one. And then on the other hand, there's Dusty, who is all about the one. And both of them are just psychedelic as all living fuck to me. It speaks to the breadth of my interest in the instrument and playing. Just holding it down - that's one side where that is completely valid and a wonderful use of the instrument, like Dusty. Just pounding on the one. And then dropping all the little other rocks they do to delineate that - dropping right back into the straight-up choogle. And all the way to Phil - obviously still the low-end of the band, but with adornments.

And you've said you went through a phase of listening to John Taylor from Duran Duran.

Yeah. Well, everybody heard that stuff, because it was so popular. He was an influence, certainly. Which goes back to an older influence - I think that guy was certainly steeped in Bernard Edwards. So, it goes back to Chic and that bass playing there - which is that funk side of stuff. Which you also have to fall on your knees at Louis Johnson's feet. The funkier side of the bass. And Bernard got to funk it up, and to get it so pop, where it's like, "What a cool use of the instrument." And John Taylor took it in the same direction - very pop, but still a fun and funky use of the bass.

There was that, and then speaking of my peers, there are a few of them - Mike Mills is another one, where I was like, "What a fun use of the bass." To completely cover the low-end, yet still have some nice, melodic accompaniment. These cool little lines - building a line around the chord. Within and around the chord.

Flea and Mike Watt were also your peers at the time.

Yeah…they're more like cohorts. Those two dudes, all of us are kind of the same person in a way. Well, Flea went on to become such a huge star. But those guys are friends of mine, and it was always these "little bass pals." Watt and I are so tight - Mike is such a fuckin' monster player. They're the guys that accepted me as a bass player, and there was something about that. Because these were guys that could really play their asses off - as far as I was concerned.

I remember hearing Flea here in town one night. I saw them play at the Mason Jar, which was this bar here in town [in Phoenix, Arizona], and Hillel [Slovak] was still in the band. And back then, Flea's tone was *so* incredible - it sounded like a synthesizer playing. Just a monster. And Mike's always been far out - from the first time I saw him, just instant kinship. He comes off stage and he's bloodied himself. Bass-centric guys - not just laying back as strictly support, but an integral part of the entirety of what the band is all about. Just a couple of bass monsters.

I've always dug the interplay between you and Curt - especially on tunes like "Maiden's Milk" and "Six Gallon Pie."

"Maiden's Milk," that one specifically - that intro part - that's a written part. Curt wrote that. I'm basically doing the same line as him at the very beginning - the thing in three. Most of what that is about is my ever-so-slight grasp of the instrument, where it's like, "Well...I can actually pull that off." That's a fairly quick line, and it needs to be played cleanly. I can pull that off. And that's picked, and it's only nominally precise - you see people who take the bass to such extreme places with their technique. But that spoke to my ability back then - to be able to at least pull off a line like that.

And then we get to the other part, that's just octaves, and then the little lines - the little walk-downs - those little "sort of funk, but not really" walk-downs to the next note and up to the next note. A really good example of that interplay that you're talking about is "Swimming Ground." Back then, Curt would have a new thing, he'd play it, and I'd play along, and then it would be like, "Well, show me what you're really doing." I remember when he showed me, "Oh, Me," I was faking it up to a point. It was like, "Show me what you're *really* doing."

So, "Swimming Ground," he had this new thing, and suddenly, there's this new cool song. He's playing it, and I'm like, "OK, he's doing something in A." Back then, my idea of the bass - the sound of it all, and what I wanted to include - that bassline just fell out. It's kind of echoing what he's doing, but it's still something that could keep me amused enough. I've never been very good at being Dusty. That guy is *so* solid - that solidity. I couldn't just go, "Duh-duh-duh-duh-duh-duh." But I'll come up with a little part that is built up inside it - a fractalized portion of something in A. Certain songs of Curt, a thing like that, it's in A, so it being a little riff thing built out of that chord - as opposed to it being a strummed thing, when he's doing these little segmented things that are building up.

Suddenly, we're making a little "construct" - he's doing these particular notes and I'm up inside of the same root note or whatever, building my little portion of it. We're building these little sculptures out of it. That was always really satisfying to me. I struggled a little bit when it hits the chords - when the verses come in. There's the little intro riff thing, and then once the chords come in, it's like, "How do you do those?" So, I would find my way through those portions. But I always felt really comfortable with the little "erector set portions" of the songs. Riff parts, too - like the beginning of "Maiden's Milk," where it's a line that needs to be played the way it goes. That kind of stuff I did real well.

You seem to have had a knack for playing P-Basses over the years.

Mostly I play P-Basses. I started out on a Jazz Bass. What really caught my eye at one point was when I finally got around to buying a bass, it was like the first year that Music Man had come out. Leo Fender had started Music Man, and I just thought they were bitching looking. I was going to buy it - I was actually to the point where I had a job. Y'know, teenager-dom, right? I found the very specific one that I wanted - that kind of dark sunburst that they had, that they first came out with - at the Arizona Music Center, this guitar shop on the west side of Phoenix. I finally got all the dough together, and there was a financing agreement that they had at the shop, where I could put down the payment, and I could get the guitar, and I could pay it off slowly.

So, I go out there to get it, and as a kid, the guy is like, "That's a nice bass, but…blah, blah, blah, blah, blah, blah." And before you knew it, I had that black Jazz Bass that I wound up doing the seven-inch [*In a Car*], *Meat Puppets I,* and *Meat Puppets II* on. He told me, "The Music Man is a nice bass…but this here is going to have more 'resale value'." And it was just straight-up bamboozle-ment - the guy just unloaded some guitar that he wanted to get rid of, when I absolutely had my eye set on the Music Man! So, I wound up with the Jazz Bass, instead.

But the cool thing about the arrangement of that place - through the finance deal, you had to take lessons for three months. So, there was a guy here, and he's still around in Phoenix, and still does lessons - Raul Tapia is his name - and as everything played out, it was very helpful to take the lessons that I took. He's the guy that taught me the neck and to know where the notes are. And the whole thing about, "As the bass player, you play the root note." He taught me about root-fifth and all that kind of stuff. Some very fundamental stuff, that was actual very helpful to learn. And I did eventually get a Music Man - a beautiful guitar. I loved that thing. It had a graphite neck - it was blonde. And one night, I was so fucked up, and I broke a string at the Peppermint Lounge [in New York City]. They had a downstairs backstage, and I went down to change the string, and I realized the strings were out in the van. And in frustration, I set my guitar down too hard, and it was one of those things - it snapped the neck, length-wise up it. Just separated the graphite. I was so distraught that I grabbed it, ran back upstairs - and this is probably about '85, y'know, we were young and everything felt lighthearted - *and I smashed the motherfucker.*

But before that, I had that Jazz Bass that I started out on, and then this guy in town had a shop, Bizarre Guitar - Bob Turner, who just passed away a couple of years ago. That's where Curt got that sunburst Les Paul that he always played, and then I got my first P-Bass, which is what I did *Up on the Sun* with. And that was a beautiful guitar. He was the guy who turned me on to EMG pickups and Badass Bridge - a certain set-up that I still dig on a P-Bass. And that was a real nice bass. I mean, *Up on the Sun* was with that, and it was a beautiful sounding guitar. And that thing, one night, I was playing at the Club Lingerie up in Los Angeles, and we got into a jammy part at the end of the set that's all goofy, and Flea was there. He comes up on stage, and he's involved in the noise-making session. I throw my guitar...and the neck breaks. And then, Flea started jumping up and down on it! It bent the truss rod.

I took the guitar back to Phoenix, and the guy Bob at Bizarre was kind of this heavy dude, and was *really* into guitars. I went into that shop in the '70s when I was first thinking about getting into bass, and that guy scared me - he was so intense. So "rock n' roll." But this was a bonding experience - I took it to him in the case, and I'm going, "This has a buzz in the neck, and I don't know why." And he goes, "Let's take a look." We open it up, and the neck is bent off in a sharp, 45-degree angle! That retired that bass, unfortunately. I always intended to get that back up and running, but never quite did. That led to my next P-Bass, which is that blue one that Curt got me, that I used for a long time.

Any words of wisdom to fellow bassists out there?

Yeah - switch to guitar! No, these days, the bass is so far out. Again, we're talking about the '70s and what got me into the bass, I went from bluegrass, and that led me to American music, and I was taken with the concept of the development of the banjo as an American instrument - one of the few things that was created here. And the amalgam that it was. And that led to jazz. I got into jazz, which led me to fusion, which led me to Jaco. Hats off to Jaco and Stanley Clarke, and the '70s era of pretty sick bass playing, which ultimately led me to rock n' roll, playing, meeting Derrick [Bostrom], punk rock, and the rest is history.

What do I say to a bass player? Fuck, obviously, I'm a proponent of playing - I still sit around and play. I tend to play more acoustic guitar - just because it's fun for me. I don't sit around and play bass as much alone. I like playing with somebody more, so I play the bass - and used to do it all the time when we all lived together. That was just a daily occurrence - to get my "playing nut" off. It's a little more chill for me to sit around and play the acoustic.

But I definitely could only encourage anybody to pick up an instrument and play - the bass or whatever - just because what it could lead to. That is why I still play. It was an "a-ha moment" that I had on the banjo. I got that after seeing the movie *Deliverance,* and decided I just had to have a banjo, got one, took lessons from a guy at a small music store up in North Phoenix, where Curt took lessons too, when we were kids - at McClarty Music. And they had a banjo instructor there. I still have the actual banjo, and on the face of it, I wrote, "Close your mouth" - because I used to sit there with my tongue hanging out when I would practice.

In bluegrass, the melody is implied by a lot of pull-offs and hammer-ons with the fifth string. One day, after practicing it, it just blew my mind that it was so cool to get to that point with the thing, that I could do that, and it just opened my head up. It was such a revelatory experience to realize that the mind was something that could be trained. That practice could lead you to whatever, which opened me up to just myself and other people, and the experience of what it was to be a person in particular. It opened me up to people *wanted* to make music - the desire to make music. And what it took to make instruments, and develop this musical vocabulary, and delved into regionalism - the different noises made by different parts of the world.

It was such a cool experience, and it's still the same thing - I still sit around and go, "Oh, look! I'm moving forward on the thing." It's such a fun companion to have. And these days, with the internet, geez, what a wide-open world. I look online sometimes, and you see like, a twelve-year-old girl someplace just playing the living fuck out of the bass. Like, "Seven Year Old Gets Down," and some kid playing some funky ass shit. So nah, I don't have nothing to say to people...*other than that.*

Les Claypool

What first attracted you to the bass?

That's sort of a two-part question - part of my attraction to the bass was the repulsion to the guitar. Years ago, when I was in junior high, there was a talent contest, and there was a band playing. I didn't know the difference between guitar and bass - I just saw that one had six strings and the other had four strings. But there were some guys playing, and there were two guitars and a drummer, and they were playing through these little Fender Champ amps on this stage in the cafeteria, and they were playing "Ramblin' Man." When the lead guitarist started doing the solo, I was like, "That is the instrument I do *not* want to play." Because it was this tinny, shrill thing, that I hated the sound of. And "that guy" turned out to be Todd Huth, who later would help me found Primus!

But for me, I would see a lot of live bands, because there were a lot of dances where I lived, and they would have live bands. I was always drawn towards the four-stringed instrument, because it just had a lower, more sultry tone to it. And then getting into a lot of funk music and whatnot, that was the focus. Whereas guitar was focused more on rock, a lot of soul and funk in the day was all bass-oriented. Plus, it only had four strings - I figured it would be easier to play.

Did you take lessons, or did you learn by playing along to records and playing with others?

I bought a bass and was instantly in a band, because everybody wanted to be Eddie Van Halen back then, so nobody wanted to play bass. So, I was instantly in a band, and there was a guy in the band...we only played original material, so he would show me how to play his songs. That was how I initially got started. But then, it was just watching players and listening. I didn't have an amp, so I would just jam along to records - not really being able to hear it, but I could get the rhythmic element of it.

Do you recall which albums you played along to most early on?

In the early days, I was a total Rush fiend, so I would just jam along with Rush. But then I got turned on to a lot of the soul and funk of the day, and started playing along with that sort of thing. But then again, I didn't have an amp, so I was just kind of "playing blind," and that's probably one reason why I play the way I do.

Since you started playing to Rush albums, I guess in a way, Geddy Lee was your bass teacher.

I don't know if I would say that. He *did* teach me a few things recently though - he was interviewing me for some book that he's working on. And I said, "OK. Part of the deal is you have to show me the proper way to play 'YYZ'." He showed me, and I had been playing it wrong all these years!

Besides Geddy, I remember you have mentioned Tony Levin, Stanley Clarke, and Chris Squire as influences. But I recently got turned on to the music of Bow Wow Wow, and their bassist, Leigh Gorman, sounded like he

may have been an influence, too. Were you a fan of his playing?

Oh yeah, of course. I was a *huge* fan. He was a monster. A lot of that scratching, and he was obviously a-thumpin' and a-pluckin' away. They were a *really* cool band. I believe their rhythm section originally came from Adam Ant. But he and the drummer [David Barbarossa] were just this powerhouse. Yeah, I was a big fan. I mean, they just didn't have much material - they only had what, two or three records? I never got to see them live, but I saw videos of him playing, and he was definitely a monster.

Which bass brand/model did you start out on?

My very first bass was a Memphis P-Bass copy.

How did you discover Carl Thompson basses and begin playing them?

I remember there was an album by Stanley Clarke, called *I Want to Play for You.* And I thought it was the coolest thing, because he had all his basses laid out on his front porch of his house, and he had a couple of Carl Thompsons on there. And I thought, "Whoa, those are *crazy* looking. They look like a piece of driftwood." And then one day, I was just at the local music store - which is what you do when you're young, you hang out at the music store and drool over all the "toys" - and there was a Carl Thompson sitting there. I picked it up and played it, and it was just like butter in my hands. So, I begged and borrowed and scrimped and saved to get that bass, and wound up getting it.

I remember you once telling me that before the Carl Thompson bass, you were playing a similar bass to what Sting was playing at the time.

I always wanted a Rickenbacker. That's the thing - I *always* wanted a Rickenbacker, like Chris Squire and Geddy Lee. I just didn't have any money. And when I finally saved up enough money to get my Rickenbacker, I went to the store, and the guy at the store talked me into this Ibanez Musician EQ, because it was supposed to be the hot new shit. It was easier to thump on than a Rick was, so I bought the Ibanez. Coincidentally, it was the same bass as Sting was playing - it's not like I bought it because of Sting.

And let's discuss your famous six-string and fretless Rainbow Bass, by Carl Thompson.

Years ago, I was working for this audio company, and one of the only times I've been to NAMM - I've only been there a couple of times - I was demoing some gear for these people. And this guy comes up to me, and says, *"Check this out,"* and he shows me this Carl Thompson six-string. I was like, "Wow...that thing is amazing!" It looked like a giant paddle. It was always my desire to eventually have a Carl Thompson six-string, so, once the band became more popular, I got ahold of Carl and we became friends, and I said, "I would love to get one of these six-strings from you." And he started making me this six-string. About halfway through, I said, "I'm going to really make it a challenge, and make it a fretless." So, he pulled all the frets out and made it a fretless for me, and that was the Rainbow Bass. [Note: The reason why it is called the "Rainbow Bass" is because it is comprised of strips of walnut, curly maple, padauk, purple heart, ebony, and cocobolo wood]

Nowadays, you mostly play your signature bass, the Pachyderm.

I loved my Carl Thompson four-string, and I have a handful of them. And they're all amazing. They're wonderful. I tell people all the time, "Look, if you're going to spend a bunch of money on a bass, buy a Carl Thompson, because they are pieces of art." He is a genius with wood. I have yet to see anybody - and I have played everything - that has the innovative craftsmanship of Carl. He's a true artist. He's the Picasso of luthiers. But the thing about Carl's basses is they're all very unique, so, I wanted something specific in a bass. He had made a few basses for me...and I don't want to tell Picasso what to paint, y'know?

So, I came up with this design based on a lot of different things - including the elements of some of the Carl Thompson basses, elements of Rickenbackers, of Jazz Basses, some of the old Turner stuff - that I like in various instruments. But then, a few innovations of my own. I am actually sitting right now in my living room, and the prototype for the Pachyderm bass is hanging on the wall. It's changed a bit since the original prototype, but basically, I took a piece of plywood, drew out a shape, cut it out, ran around with it, made another one, then Dan Maloney - who I have known since high school, and has made my Banjo Bass and he made an upright years ago - made me another prototype, and I carved on it and did a bunch of woodwork on it. I mean, it was just a blank - and then he made the prototype. I cranked on it a bit, and I've been evolving it since then.

But the whole notion is I want it to be like a Ferrari - I want it to be something that not only looks amazing, but is comfortable, ergonomic, and you get that feeling of butter - like when whatever you are thinking just comes out in your hands, and you don't have to struggle with it. They're very easy-to-play instruments.

You just mentioned the Banjo Bass.

I've always loved the banjo, and years ago, I thought, "Hey, let's put a bass neck on a banjo, and I can go ding-dica-dong, ding-dica-dong." So, I asked Dan to do it, and he made the Banjo Bass for me. It's an amazing thing.

You are one of the few bassists that utilizes a tremolo bar on some of your instruments.

Basically, years ago, I saw Stanley Clarke had an Alembic that had a Bigsby tremolo bar on it. And I just thought it was the coolest thing. So, I used to work for this audio company, and I noticed that Kahler had made this tremolo bar for basses, so I got one. I had my buddy Dan - who makes all my basses - stick it on my Carl Thompson, and it just went from there.

Any advice about keeping a bass in tune that has a tremolo bar?

It just does *not* like to stay in tune. That's why I play in Primus - it doesn't necessarily matter so much if you stay in tune! Tuning is an abstract concept. Being in tune is subjective. I mean, there are different things you can do - when you get the feel for the instrument, you can bend the strings back into tune. You've just got to keep an eye on it.

What do you recall about coming up with the bassline to "Tommy the Cat"?

I always liked playing with players - drummers-wise - that emphasized sixteenth notes. I wanted something that just rumbled through. So, that's what the bassline to "Tommy the Cat" is - just rumbling through. There's no real pauses or breaks in the part. It's a steady sixteenth note rumble. It's like a train. And I remember I was playing with this woman at the time in this little side band - I played that thing for her, and she was like, "Oh my God, that sounds like a locomotive."

Did it take a while to be able to sing and play that bassline together?

Yeah. I had the bassline for a while, and then I had this whole "Say baby" thing in my head, and this character of Tommy the Cat - which was loosely based on somebody I used to be in a band with. I decided those two things *have to* go together. So, I forced them together, and it took me a while to play it and sing it at the same time. It's one of those things where you've got to get them both into your subconscious, so you're not thinking about it - it just happens.

Are there any songs difficult to sing and play?

Oh, there's lots of them. [Laughs] There are just *songs* that are hard to play. People always ask me, "Why don't you play 'DMV'?" *Because it's fucking hard!* [Laughs] That's a hard-ass song to play. Some things you go the extra mile for when you're young, and then you realize that you've painted yourself into a bit of a corner. And definitely, "DMV" is one of those songs. I mean, I *can* play it - we did *Pork Soda* in its entirety for one of the New Year's shows a couple years back. But man, it's a bitch. It definitely takes some work.

What about coming up with the bassline to "Jerry Was a Race Car Driver"?

That was something we were just kind of jamming, and I started doing my "Tony Levin thing." One of the things that I did with the six-string was I always liked what Tony did with the Stick. All the people call it "the tapping thing" - I'm just trying to do what Tony Levin did with the Stick. [Laughs] But the Stick - to me - was just this confusing octopus. I'd look at it, and go, "What the hell am I supposed to do with that thing?" So, I just sort of applied some of the stuff I would see him do on my six-string.

Did you ever try to play a Chapman Stick?

I've never even held one. It's like keyboards - I get on a keyboard, and I go, "Eh...what the hell do I do?" I sit there and play circus music on it, and that's about it.

And what about the bassline to "My Name Is Mud"?

I was actually sitting backstage at the Greek Theatre in Berkeley, and I was playing my bass - just sitting there, fiddling around. And I started playing this line, but I was playing it like, twice as fast. I remember my dad sitting there, going, *"What the hell are you doing?"* It just stuck with me. And I don't remember when, but at some point in time, I played it with the guys, and we started slowing it down, and it became what it became. But, it started out as almost just a warm-up exercise.

Lastly, what are some of your favorite basslines to play?

I'm not big on favorites, but one of my all-time favorite basslines to play - of anybody's - is the Tony Levin line for [King Crimson's] "Thela Hun Ginjeet." And it's funny - I never read reviews or blogs or any of that stuff, because I can read all kinds of wonderful things, and then, it just takes one negative thing to bum me out. I would be a terrible politician...*because I'm a sensitive man.*

So, I was reading something online - I can't remember where it was - and I read, "I can't listen to Frog Brigade's version of 'Thela Hun Ginjeet,' because Les is playing it wrong." And I was like, "Godammit! I can't win!" So then, I started watching this video of Tony playing "Thela Hun Ginjeet" - a live Crimson thing - and I *had* been playing it wrong this whole time! [Laughs] So, I love that line - even though I played it wrong for quite a while. Now, *hopefully I am playing it correctly.*

Other Books By
Greg Prato

Music:

A Devil on One Shoulder and an Angel on the Other: The Story of Shannon Hoon and Blind Melon

Touched by Magic: The Tommy Bolin Story

Grunge Is Dead: The Oral History of Seattle Rock Music

No Schlock...Just Rock! (A Journalistic Journey: 2003-2008)

MTV Ruled the World: The Early Years of Music Video

The Eric Carr Story

Too High to Die: Meet the Meat Puppets

The Faith No More & Mr. Bungle Companion

Overlooked/Underappreciated: 354 Recordings That Demand Your Attention

Over the Electric Grapevine: Insight into Primus and the World of Les Claypool

Punk! Hardcore! Reggae! PMA! Bad Brains!

Iron Maiden: '80 '81

Survival of the Fittest: Heavy Metal in the 1990s

Scott Weiland: Memories of a Rock Star

German Metal Machine: Scorpions in the '70s

The Other Side of Rainbow

Shredders!: The Oral History of Speed Guitar (And More)

The Yacht Rock Book: The Oral History of the Soft, Smooth Sounds of the 60s, 70s, and 80s

100 Things Pearl Jam Fans Should Know & Do Before They Die

Sports:

Sack Exchange: The Definitive Oral History of the 1980s New York Jets

Dynasty: The Oral History of the New York Islanders, 1972- 1984

Just Out of Reach: The 1980s New York Yankees

The Seventh Year Stretch: New York Mets, 1977-1983

38185545R00144

Made in the USA
Middletown, DE
06 March 2019